CONTENT WRITING PROFITS

Steps for Writing Online Content and Replacing Your Day Job with the Income

D.L. Hughes

Content Writing Profits

*Steps for Writing Online Content and
Replacing Your Day Job with the Income*

Published by Box City Books - San Diego, California

Copyright © 2018 by D.L. Hughes – VelocityWriting.com

ISBN: 978-1-98-321738-8

No part of this book may be reproduced in any form or by any electronic or mechanical means including information storage and retrieval systems, without permission in writing from the author. The only exception is by a reviewer, who may quote short excerpts in a review. See complete legal notices, disclaimers, and disclosures at the end of this book. [R2]

If you gain benefit from this book, please leave a review. Thank you.

Don't miss the BONUS SECTION at the end of this book. There is information that will help you reach your writing goals.

Writing Books by D.L. Hughes

The Self-Publishing Trap
Look Before You Leap into the Pay-to-Publish World

Write Fast, Write Well
Velocity Writing Tools and Techniques

Writing Books is Easy, Selling Books is Hard
Straight Talk About How To Sell Your Book

7 Essential Hacks for Fiction Writers
Enhance Your Novel with Professional Techniques

See latest writing book releases at VelocityWriting.com/books/

Online Writing Courses by D.L. Hughes

Motivation Secrets for Writers
How to Speed Write Your Book with Voice Recognition Software
How to Get Profitable Book Ideas
How to Get Kindle Reviews the Fast, Effective and Legal Way
How to Write an Effective Promotional News Release

See latest course releases at VelocityWriting.com/online-courses/

Dedicated to the many writers I have mentored over the years who have aspired to make money with their craft.

CONTENTS

What You'll Discover 1

: Part One: Earn What You're Worth 3

1 What Is Content Writing? 4

2 An Early Warning About Content Mills 10

3 Profitable Places to Make Money 18

4 Common Content Writing Rates 24

: Part Two : The Content Writing Process 28

5 Word Count is Important 29

6 Narrowing the Topic 33

7 General Content Writing Guide 38

8 A Proven Writing Pattern 44

9 How To Do Fast Research 50

10 How To Be an Original Writer 57

11 How to Be Interesting 67

12 Be SEO Aware 73

13 Revision and Editing 78

: Part Three : Building Your Business 86

14 Best Places to Find Clients 87

15 How Much Should You Charge? 93

16 Collecting Your Fee 103

17 How to Increase Your Client Base 108

18 How to Increase Income from Existing Clients 112

19 Should You Sign Legal Agreements? 117

20 Taking Care of Business 121

Meet the Author 125

Bonus Section 126

Legal Notices, Disclaimers & Disclosures 127

End Notes – Resources 130

WHAT YOU'LL DISCOVER

Do you know how many websites there are? Over 1 billion! And that's up by about 150 million over the previous year.[1] They all share one common factor. Each one has content. This offers a real opportunity for enterprising writers.

Everyone is trying to attract attention to their website or blog. They want to increase traffic to their site.

They want to show up near the top on search engine page rankings so people will click and go to their page.

Importantly, they want to sell products, services or ideas to site visitors.

However, content writing is more than just writing articles or blog posts or other copy. It includes email newsletters, social media posts, news releases, and product descriptions. YouTube style videos and podcasts are becoming increasingly popular, and content writers script them in many cases.

Content writers write material that people read, see and hear. Most content jobs are 1,500 words or less, regardless of the form they take.

The focus of this book is on writing blog posts. It's a transferable concept. When you master blog posts, you can adapt the style to all the other forms of content writing I mentioned.

> *Content, in the way we discuss it, has one common factor—it is website-driven writing.*

In all cases, your job as a content writer is to inform and persuade. You want to do that in an entertaining way.

You can turn that skill into a profitable full-time business if you wish. That entire process — the writing and the business development— is what this book is about.

: PART ONE:
EARN WHAT YOU'RE WORTH

1
WHAT IS CONTENT WRITING?

Content writing is more than sitting down and expressing yourself off the top of your head. Let's look at five key points which make content writing unique.

Before we get into the details, let me mention the difference between a post and an article. Places like LinkdIn.com make a distinction, but there's no distinction in this book because they both serve the same purpose. Length and focus may vary slightly, but both are pieces of writing. That's why I use post and article interchangeably.

CONTENT DEFINED

Content, in the way I'm talking about it, is material that is Internet-related. It appears on websites in almost all cases. It is:

- Blog posts (Articles)

- Email newsletters

- Social media posts

- News releases
- Product descriptions
- Video or podcast scripts

The connection is that they are almost entirely web-related.

But content is mostly highly focused blog posts or website pages. When you're able to write posts—as I emphasize—you will have the skills to write all the rest. You'll get transferable concepts in this book.

This kind of content is written to entertain, inform or persuade, and you ring the bell when you do all three at once. Content sells products, services or ideas to site visitors. Let's look at some basic elements of this kind of writing.

THE CHARACTERISTICS OF CONTENT WRITING

I'm going to tell you *how* to do the following things in later sections. Right now, I want to define the characteristics of content writing, and it applies to all the different types I just mentioned.

IT IS WRITTEN TO A SPECIFIC LENGTH

Content is written to a specific length. It's not like a novel where you just keep writing until your story is told.

Word count is important. You want each word to have significance.

This applies to blog posts and all other kinds of content I mentioned. Each kind has its own preferred length. This is so important I give an entire chapter to this.

IT ADDRESSES A SPECIFIC NEED

You don't want to write globally — you want to be narrowly focused. You want to be specific.

Let's have a little example. Someone asks you to write about aspirin? You don't want to write about aspirin in general. You want to focus down and be specific.

You should be able to write 25 or more different 500-word articles on the different aspects of an aspirin, for example:

- How the pain reliever was discovered would be one article.

- Individual articles on the people who discovered it would be other articles.

- There would be an article on the Bayer company who controlled the formula for many decades.

- There could be an article on the formula itself, perhaps a different article on each ingredient.

- You could write an article about when aspirin became popular.

- You could write separately on some of the side-effects of aspirin. And so forth.

See what I'm saying? When you write content, you focus on one particular aspect of the topic. You are specific. You want to keep what you have to say fluff-free. Don't stray away from the main point you intend to make.

IT FOLLOWS A PARTICULAR PATTERN

Content writing follows a particular pattern. Parts go together in a specific way. There's a method. To be successful, you must follow that method.

People read online articles differently than they do print articles and so that pattern becomes very important to the way you write them. Yes, we'll be looking at this pattern in detail in one of our chapters.

IT IS WRITTEN IN A FAST, ACCURATE WAY

If you're going to make money, you need to know how to do fast, accurate research and to write quickly as well.

You don't want to waste time by over-researching your topic, but you want to provide reliable, factual information. Productivity is important to your success.

IT ATTRACTS THE INTEREST OF READERS

Above all, no matter what you are trying to convey to your readers, you have an obligation to be interesting. Nobody reads boring content.

CAN YOU WRITE IN THIS WAY?

Is this a difficult kind of writing? No. Anyone can learn the skill. Can you write like this? Yes, I think so. You can either be a new, aspiring writer or an established one. In either case, there is a market for your writing.

Now, you can't make serious money writing an occasional article for $5 or $10. To succeed, you'll need a steady flow of work at a decent fee.

If you can research and write 3,000 or more words per day—which is common for a professional—you can likely make six figures each year or far more. But you need a businesslike approach to build a client base.

It takes time and effort to develop a client base. A solid client base is composed of repeat clients who pay well.

I know, you just want to write! Operating a business isn't any fun! I have sections in this book that offer a recipe for finding the kind of clients you need to sustain a high income.

CONTENT WRITING IS ABOUT GETTING RESULTS

Your entire purpose is to get your readers to respond in an affirmative way.[2] There are different kinds of what are called, "conversions."

- Increased page views
- Visitors on pages longer
- Motivate them to download ebooks or other content
- Get them to sign-up for email newsletters
- Get them to respond to special offers
- Trigger a sales conversation online or by phone
- Make an immediate purchase

Your content should generate reader action. That's the point of it.

* * *

There are many literary forms. Some people like to write poetry, novels, or nonfiction books. Content writing is a distinct literary form and can be just as important as any other kind.

Like all good literary forms, content writing appears before the eyes of a reader who is in a particular state of mind and then seeks to change that state. All literature influences people, even when it appears only to entertain. All writers are engaged in the process of changing the way people think.

Content writing is a legitimate short-form writing genre. You can change lives with blog posts and articles. You may think an article is just a drop of water in the endless Internet sea, but the reality is that each article has the potential to change a life in ways small or large.

Content writing can be an adventure. You'll work with interesting people, help others and be a change agent. You'll learn new things and have the potential to make serious money.

2
AN EARLY WARNING ABOUT CONTENT MILLS

Previously, I defined content writing. I said there are over 1 billion websites out there that need content. So it would seem like there is a lot of opportunity. Now, I want to be more specific about those moneymaking opportunities for content writers.

Before we look at the opportunities, it's necessary to talk about one of the greatest pitfalls that could derail your content writing career at the start. Content Mills are common and some content writers, especially new ones, think they are a good option for making money. I think not. It's important to discuss early, then, I'll discuss more sensible and profitable content writing opportunities in the next chapter.

THE PERIL OF CONTENT MILLS

What is a content mill and why are they a bad choice, in my professional opinion, for content writers?

A content mill is a site like Upwork.com, Freelancer.com or Textbroker.com who acts as an intermediary between writer and clients.

You sign-up, abide by their policies, bid on work at low rates, and then you pay them a commission and fees for brokering your work. To make money, you must grind out lots of writing at cheap prices.

I've only named three such sites, but there are many hundreds of them, and they're pretty much the same in terms of what they do and how they do it.

By the way, there are some content writing mills that make writers pay upfront money to get jobs, such as a membership. The regular content mills that I'm talking about in this chapter are bad enough. But those that require an advance fee to get freelance jobs are really the worst of the worst in my opinion.

NEVER pay to get a writing job, even if it's bundled with other services. Expect a scam. You don't need to pay an advance fee to get writing jobs. Ever.

Do content mills serve a helpful purpose for content writers? I don't think so.

- They are magnets for clients who want to pay you pennies per word.

- They attract huge numbers of writers willing to be exploited by these clients.

    Many writers who work for content mills don't realize they're being exploited. For example, people in underdeveloped countries can buy groceries for their family for a week if they get $5 for their work.

    In developed countries, $5 doesn't mean much. That money barely buys a box of cereal much less the milk to put on it.

There are all kinds of sweatshops; some work for pennies an hour sewing clothes, others work for pennies per word. Same thing. It's tragic.

- Most of the content mills have policies in place that keep you from maximizing your income. For example, you must reach certain levels of productivity before you're entitled to get a decent pay rate. Also, they take a huge bite out of your already small income; some take 25% or more of your income for their services.

- They control when, and if, you get paid. You are subject to their policies. There are plenty of complaints online about people having payments withheld for bogus reasons. Or people dropped as writers for no stated reason and without getting the money they already earned. The content mill is the puppet master and writers are the puppets.

- One of the worst features of a content mill is that they create a barrier to free and open communication between you and your client. You see, the client is *their* client, not *your* client, so they maintain control by filtering any conversation through their site.

Real freelancers develop a relationship with their own clients. That is essential to a successful content writing business.

So, you're not really a freelancer if you work for a content mill. You become more like an indentured slave to them. Am I alone in my views? No.

CASE HISTORIES OF CONTENT MILLS ABUSING WRITERS

Carol Tice started a blog called MakeALivingWriting.com because she disliked low-paying content mills.[3] She's done a lot of reliable research. She interviews both the people who run the content mills and those who write for them.

She interviewed one content mill client that paid $100 for multi-page websites. Carol told him that she was paid three times that for a single article.

He said, "That's way too much."

I'd say Carol Tice nailed it when she told him, "Maybe in the Philippines those kind of rates work, bud, but it's hard to live off that in the First World."

Carol also interviews people who have written for content mills. One of them, Jennifer Roland, said of Textbroker.com:

> I wrote one piece for Textbroker at $.05 cents per word. I have never gone back to write enough to meet the minimum threshold for payout, so they still owe me $1.50. I chalked it up to a life lesson and went on to find real clients that pay real money.[4]

That's a pretty fair picture of the content mill landscape in my view. As a writer, you need to do what is called "due diligence" to check the offers people or companies make. You don't want to get caught in one of the many traps in the content writing world. You never want to become an unwitting victim of someone's moneymaking scheme.

There is a hidden problem with content mill sites. Clients are blind to it, and it's hurting them. Content writers cannot ignore it. Let's look at that.

THE PROBLEM OF CROSS-CULTURAL COMMUNICATION

Clients seem to have no knowledge of "cross-cultural communication." They usually don't know good writing from bad—all they know is cheap—so they accept writing from people on that basis, even though English is not their first language. An article may make sense (although many don't), but the words are lifeless because they contain little or no cultural nuance.

By the way, I'm not picking on people just because English is not their first language. I'm picking on everyone who writes in a language, not their own first language and has not immersed themselves for an extended time (10 years or so) in the culture where that language is spoken.

Cross-cultural communication is a two-way street. North American writers, no matter what university they went to, should probably not be writing content for any individual or company in an underdeveloped country.

For example, English is my first language. I have never been to India. Therefore, I'd say it's completely crazy for me to try to write convincing content in Hindi (the main native language of India) even though I might have studied Hindi in university.

You have to be inside a language and culture to gain insight into the thought processes of the people. There is no substitute for that.

IDIOMATIC LANGUAGE IS ESSENTIAL

Idiomatic language uses expressions that are natural to a native speaker no matter what that language may be. In this book, we're using English as the native language by way of example.

Just because people have learned English in school in another culture does not mean they have mastered idiomatic American or British English. Since that is the case, it means they are a liability to clients, not an asset to them. Some clients need to be educated about cross-cultural communication. They are getting cheap writing, but they don't get the kind of writing that reaps the benefits they desire.

No matter where you live, write in your own language using all the cultural cues native to your own culture.

Using idiomatic English is especially important when it comes to writing persuasive content. You can't persuade people if you are unaware of the trigger words that result in action.[5]

The thing that all content clients should know is that cheap offshore content will probably not result in sales. The writing may be readable, but if it's not idiomatic, the persuasive power is drained from it. You can help educate prospective clients about that reality.

WRITE FOR YOUR OWN CULTURE

Now, all this is the long way to say that companies like Upwork.com offer content writing opportunities, but it largely depends on where you live and where your customer lives if results are to be mutually beneficial. Language is important of course, but all language is based on discrete cultural understanding. That cultural understanding is the "language beneath the language." It is the verbal "wink and nod."

Also, it's difficult to build and maintain a client base if you are constantly dealing with cross-cultural communication issues. People outside a culture, like those in underdeveloped countries who want to work in other cultures, are almost totally dependent on services like Upwork.com, Freelancer.com or Textbroker.com because they can't handle the business side themselves. They need an intermediary for that. The same would be true for you if you were a North American trying to develop business in Paraguay or Pakistan or any other culture.

If you're going to use a company like Upwork.com or Freelancer.com and hope to make a living through their services, then you need to understand both the cultural and the competitive landscape. If you want to grow your content writing business, you'll want to say inside the boundaries of your native language and culture.

* * *

Let me conclude by saying that you want to avoid marketplaces like Upwork.com, Freelancer.com or Textbroker.com where cheap clients throw loose change at people who don't mind or are unable to avoid, being exploited.

Bidding on jobs at places like this can lead to bad experiences. Yes, some people do it. You'll work long and hard at such places but not see worthwhile results in most cases.

Many people in the content mill grind come to believe they can make more money as content writers elsewhere. They are correct. In my view, the negatives are so strong that I'd don't think the content mills even serve as a good place for new writers to get started. There are far better ways to get started, and I mention them later.

Experience has taught me that content writers are better off taking the time and effort to build a real freelance content writing business where people value your work and are willing to pay you for it. I discuss that in the next chapter.

Some people will tell you they have found success working for content mills. Maybe so. The choice is yours.

3
PROFITABLE PLACES TO MAKE MONEY

There are many ways to make content writing money. You do not need to rely on the content mills. What are some of those options?

A PROFESSIONAL APPROACH

Professional freelancing is when you develop your own client base. You cater to their needs, and they value your work. You provide high-quality writing, and they pay you professional prices.

It's true that you have to get clients, but it can be very lucrative when you do it right.

I have an entire section dedicated to where and how to find clients in this book, but I'd like you to start thinking about the importance of this now.

You don't want to get into the trap of finding a new client, writing one article, and then start looking for another client. You want to build your own stable of clients.

While you must start with one client at a time, you can't build a business without repeat customers or writing multiple posts at one time — bulk jobs.

You keep developing your client base until you have a group of clients that need your work, appreciate how you do it, and are willing to pay you what you're worth.

For many years, I had a dozen clients that supplied me with an excellent income. I seldom had to find new clients. My stable of clients kept me busy and my bank account fat. So, the shortest path to content writing success is by developing a solid client base, and I teach that in this book.

Keep in mind that as a professional, you want always to increase your sphere of influence and work to get more profitable writing jobs. In later chapters, I discuss how to find profitable clients, how to increase your client base, how much to charge and how to earn more money per client. Each of these are important because there are only so many hours in the day, and you must work wisely and efficiently to reach your income goals.

Some people suggest that you must hire others to do the writing if you want to make a large income. You get the work, assign it to people who are willing to work cheaply. Then you edit it and collect the fee from the client. This makes no sense to me. You are no longer a writer but have become the owner of a mini-content mill. You are managing groups of clients, writers, and articles, and that's as thankless as trying to herd cats.

If you want to be a writer, then you want to write and manage your jobs and your time in a profitable way. But running a mini-content mill is not the same as being a writer. They are two far different occupations.

BE YOUR OWN CLIENT

As a writer, you have the power to create your own blog or series of blogs. You pick the topic and write all the content.

Writers make serious money by supplying content to their own site. You don't get paid for each blog post as you would do if you were freelancing, but you write to build traffic to your website.

The more traffic you get—the more site visitors— the more money you make.

How do you make money when you supply content to your own blog or website? It comes from:

- Advertising

- Affiliate offers

- Selling your own products and services

- Support payments from fans who love your work. Patreon.com makes this easier than ever.

What is the easiest way to generate income? Advertising and affiliate offers if your site has a lot of traffic. Patreon if you have a large and dedicated fan base. What is the most profitable? It's not easy as the other options, but selling your own products (like books and online courses) or services (consulting, writing or whatever you do) will be your major profit center.

In normal freelancing, you use content writing techniques to build traffic and get customers for others. In this case, you're using the same techniques to build your own business.

The amazing thing is that many millions are succeeding! It takes lots of hard work, but a successful blog can be a road to riches. Millions of people are receiving income from their blogging efforts.

MOVE INTO MULTIMEDIA

Another profit path— use your writing skills to create a video channel or a podcast.

You use the same blog writing principles, but you tailor them for the voice. You make your scripts ear-friendly and conversational. Never make it sound like you're reading. Add the dynamics of your voice and personality to your scripts.

You still want a website, but you design your video channel or podcast to drive traffic to it.

WRITE VIDEO SCRIPTS AND PRODUCE THEM

You don't need lots of expensive cameras, lights and microphones today like in the past. Some people make money using newer smartphones—their audio and video can be great for starting out when you use them correctly.

You make money the same way with videos as with blog posts, that is, advertising, affiliate offers and selling your own products and services. You can use sites like YouTube for ad income displayed there and to drive traffic to your blog.

However, YouTube is constantly changing the rules. It's harder to make money off ads alone there than ever before. Every change they make seems to be one step forward and two steps back.

For example, not long ago you could make money from YouTube ads. But there were some bad actors who posted anti-social material, and so they penalized everyone by limiting who could monetize their videos with ads. It seemed like an irrational act and those just starting out were punished for the most part, not the people who had huge followings.

Lots of video people started to use Patreon.com to accept income from grateful fans to make up for lost ad income. YouTube didn't like that, so they started their own Patreon-like program where fans can pay $4.99 per month to support content creator channels. That might have been a step forward, but the two steps back is that it's still for the high rollers. You need a minimum of 100,000 subscribers to qualify. That's a lot. And also, YouTube takes a 30% cut of your income.[6]

You have to jump through lots of hoops to please the YouTube Police. That's why you want to use YouTube videos to drive traffic to your own site.

There are three YouTube gurus that offer lots of sensible advice, and I have supplied links to them. They keep on top of trends. You can trust them, and I suggest you hear what they have to say before you enter this field as a content writer.[7]

WRITE AND PRODUCE A PODCAST

Podcasts are growing like crazy. They are like on-demand radio shows, and they're available on every topic imaginable. Many have huge listening audiences.

You write a script, which you record in mp3 format, and use free software like Audacity to edit it. Then, you post it on Apple iTunes and the scores of other podcast sites, and people download or stream and listen to your content.

When your podcast gets popular, you may be invited to join one of the podcast networks which generates ad income for you. As always, however, the money comes from advertising, affiliate income, Patreon donations or the sales of your own products or services.

* * *

To tie this together, let me remind you can make money in several ways.

- You can make money as a freelancer with your own client base. You are writing for others, and they pay you by the word.

- You can make money by content writing to draw traffic to your own blog.

- You can write and produce your own videos or podcasts—or both. They are increasingly popular and can be very profitable.

No matter what method, or combination of methods you use, they all start with content-style writing.

4
COMMON CONTENT WRITING RATES

This book is about writing online content. Such content is designed to inform, persuade and entertain. Once you learn to do that, you can transfer the concept to other kinds of content writing, including video and audio scripts and the other types of content I've mentioned.

But the core skill is mastering the content writing form and method. Then, your job is to build your own loyal client list from there. You will build a career by working for that group of people.

You can have a very stable working life and a great income when you build your own client base. That's where the gold is for content writers.

OVERVIEW: WHAT ARE YOUR SKILLS WORTH?

How much should you be making as a content writing freelancer with your own client base?

Well, not the pennies per word offered by the content mills.

I share the methods for computing income in the business section below. There are many factors involved in how much you charge when you have your own client base, so that's why there's a whole section about the right strategies for that.

But now, let's look at the raw rates that professional content writers use as a factor to set their rates.

There are people who will want to pay you pennies per word. They can't write in most cases, so they try to make profits off your skills. The crazy thing is that most of these types of clients don't know good writing from bad. They are the worst possible type of client.

I suppose that some writers will always be willing to be enslaved to such clients, but offering pennies per word—and writing for pennies per word—is a cycle of shame.

In my view, everyone deserves to be properly compensated for their skills. And many clients are offering honest compensation. Let's see what the real standard is in this overview.

RETAIL RATES

Writer's Market has a schedule of prices for different kinds of writing jobs.[8] I would consider their pricing to be "retail." A standard price, no discounts.

How much do they suggest you get for web content writing? The low is 35 cents per word. The high is $1.25—that's US dollars—per word. The average charge is 86 cents per word. That's for general writing and specialty writing commands more.

This is what writers like you and I get, not the 2 or even 5 cents per word in the race to the bottom and to bankruptcy offered by so many low-budget entrepreneurs.

WHOLESALE RATES

There's another group called the Editorial Freelancers Association the-efa.org, and they have their own schedule of fees.

If *Writer's Market* is "Retail" pricing, this is more like "Wholesale" pricing. What is their range for general writing? From 20 cents to $2 per word.

You can see the range on their chart[9] for various specialties. Fiction and Grants and Proposals are listed, but they are not content writing in the way we've defined it. Grants and Proposals are far different than Sales/PR so that may confuse some people.

In any event, the 1,000-word article you write should be worth between $200 and $2,000 depending on your experience level, your client and the topic, even at these wholesale rates.

The truth be known, you will need to personalize your rates, and I explain how to do that in the "Building Your Business" section. On a practical level, rates vary by skill level, region, the market niche, and other factors. All content writers need to adjust their fees based on these factors and not try to be known for being the cheapest writer around.

* * *

Here's the big idea to keep in mind. If you are a professional writer, then your work has value. Yet, there are too many writers that are desperate for income and will work for pennies per word. And there are plenty of clients who are more than willing to exploit those writers.

I'm suggesting in this book that content writing opportunities are huge. You can get paid properly for your expert skills.

Let me cement the idea that your writing has value in this little story.

Back in the early 1840s when American writer Edgar Alan Poe was an unknown—long before he became famous — he was writing for 3 cents per word. Quote the Raven: "That's not much forevermore...."

Accounting for inflation since then, he would be getting 94 cents per word today. No raise for merit, just inflation see the point here? Some are still offering a few pennies per word to writers. Goofy, isn't it?

You don't need to write for beggar wages. Good writers have value. Find decent clients to get paid what you're worth. There are many good clients out there.

: PART TWO :

THE CONTENT WRITING PROCESS

5
WORD COUNT IS IMPORTANT

You may think that it's odd that I start the content writing process with a chapter on word count. The reality is, word count is the foundation of everything you write for two main reasons:

- Word count determines the amount of money you receive. It's about how many words you can write in a specific time.

- It determines the structure of your article, the information you choose to include in it and your reader response to it.

Even if you charge an hourly fee—a bad idea in my view—you base that fee on your productivity. No matter how much time you spend in getting clients or research and writing, it all boils down to how much you write. Reason enough to focus early on word count.

THE ARITHMETIC OF PROFIT

When it comes to writing blog posts, I see some of those low-end ads that say: "$10 for a 600 to 800-word article."

That's chump change, of course, but do you see the trap? They want to pay you the same fee for an article that has a 200-word difference.

The basic payment for 600 words is 1.6 cents per word. But it drops to 1.2 cents per word if you write 800 words.

If 600 words are worth 1.6 cents, why would it be worth only 1.2 cents per word for more work? Believe me; these shady clients will want 800 words for their $10.

The fact is, if you multiply the 1.6 cent rate times 800 words, you'll see that you should get a little over $13. Does $3 make any difference? Absolutely! It adds up, and it adds up quickly.

Say you write 10- 500-word articles per day. That's $80 at that terrible 1.6 cent rate. If they were 800 words, you should earn $128. Are you prepared to give away $48 every day because you don't charge by the word? I hope not.

By the way, I used this 1.6 cent example because it's common. It's an example of how low-paying clients want to pay chump change and still exploit writers. I don't recommend you work for such a low rate.

The first lesson of content writing. Word count is important. You must be paid fairly for every word you write.

Any other option is likely to lead you to failure because your pace of writing is at the core of your income.

As a content writer, like everyone else, you only have so many hours in the day. You need to make your time count. You can't afford to give away 200 words.

As you become more experienced, you'll see that your time and your word count are intertwined and are essential to making money.

WORD COUNT AND ARTICLE STRUCTURE

Let's look at why word count also determines the structure of your article. I'll be going into detail later about how to write an article, but at this point, I want to talk about the characteristics of a well-written article. Please bear with me as I unfold the full process.

When I was a young editor at a national magazine, my boss told me he wanted me to write "tight and bright." That's kind of an old journalism cliché. What does it mean?

To "write tight" means that you eliminate the fluff. You want every word to count. You want each word to target the brain of the reader like a light beam. You say everything for a reason. You don't wander or use unnecessary words to expand word count. You eliminate all those pesky adverbs, for example, as you aim for maximum clarity.

To "write bright" simply means to put the emphasis on the more upbeat aspect of any story. That's always a good approach. People are looking for solutions, and content writers supply them.

In this context, our focus is on writing tight.

Here's the point. When you know your word count in advance, you are able to allocate words by section—your headers and sub-headers.

- You can allocate time to research each idea you're expressing.

- Having a word count forces you to increase the clarity of the points you want to make.

- A word count helps you eliminate the fluff that readers hate and increases clarity.

- It helps you make more money by writing more efficiently.

How many words go into an a blog article or other content? That depends on the assignment. Generally content of the type we're talking about in this book runs from about 500 to 1,500 words, but more details about that later.

* * *

I hope you see that word count is the foundation of your content writing career. When people read web articles, they expect tightly written information. They don't want fluff. They want you to get to the point with details that hold their interest.

Count every word and make every word count.

How you structure your content determines the value of your writing both in terms of speed and quality. You want to know the word count before you start writing. Word count is the foundation of your content writing success.

6
NARROWING THE TOPIC

This chapter is far more important than it may seem at first. Why? Because content writing is about being specific. The idea of being specific is lost on many people. Most tend to be vague and speak in general ways, and that often transfers into their writing.

I touched on how you can isolate different aspects of a topic when I talked about aspirin earlier. Now I want to take you to a different place. This is about writing about a specific topic in a specific way. It's about how to develop one clearly defined central idea.

YOU CAN'T BE VAGUE WHEN YOU WRITE CONTENT

Let's look at an example of what I mean. A client may ask you to write an article on the real estate market. But that's not good enough. There are probably 100,000 aspects of the real estate market, and you need to know precisely what aspect the client is interested in. Once you know that you are able to structure your article properly.

Having a laser focus at the start helps you write quality material quickly. It puts money in your bank account because you are not floundering around trying target what you want and need to say. You just get to it.

YOUR CLIENT GETS YOU STARTED

Your client narrows "real estate" and asks you to write about one aspect, and that's mortgages. But still, that's not enough for a content writer to do his or her best work.

Why? Because there are many aspects of mortgages—everything from:

- Defining what they are
- Where to apply for one
- Qualification requirements
- The paperwork involved
- The interest rate
- Repayment schedules
- ... and scores of other aspects

New writers want to "go wide" and cover many aspects of the topic in one article. Seasoned professionals know better—they don't want to go wide, they want to go deep. They explore one central idea in an article. They address one issue or solve one problem. That approach is very attractive to readers.

DRILL DOWN ON ONE CENTRAL IDEA

Let's use a home mortgage example. We'll pick one narrow aspect: "The Best Place to Get a Home Mortgage." That will be our title.

It's specific and offers the hope of a solution for people thinking about buying a new home. My brief outline would look like this:

- Introduction (Hook) - Getting a good deal on your new loan will save you thousands of dollars over the term of the mortgage. Show statistics.

- Point 1 - Best places to get a mortgage if you are a first time home buyer.

- Point 2 - Best online mortgage lenders.

- Point 3 - Best mortgage lenders if you have bad credit.

- Conclusion (Call-to-Action). This is a summation of your key ideas but, importantly, it has a call-to-action. You want people to act. More about that in a later chapter.

By the way, I could have written an entire article on EACH of the three points, and with experience, you can too.

But notice in my example that I stayed on topic. There's no fluff and no drift away from the focus. I fulfilled the promise of the title. I went deep, not wide. That's the mark of a well-written article that will interest your reader. It will help your client get the results he or she wants.

I talked about word count in the last chapter. This example article, which has a specific focus, is an easy 1,000 words if that's what your client is paying you for. That's a 125-word introduction, 250 words for each point and a 125-word call-to-action conclusion.

That kind of precision is how you make money with content writing. You must narrow the topic before you start.

Let me give you one additional tip that I think you'll find valuable.

MAKE YOUR CLIENT WORK HARDER

Your client gets you started, and you narrow the topic. But a real secret to success is to get the client to narrow the topic for you. Let me explain why.

If he or she gives you a general topic and you go ahead and write about it, I can almost guarantee that you will not meet their expectations.

They will want you to rewrite what you have done. You want to avoid rewrites as much as possible because you can't make money writing for some ultra-picky client.

Why will they want you to do rewrites? Because they don't know what they want in the first place. I go into this whole issue in detail later.

At this point, you must determine in advance what your client is seeking. The best way to do that is to ask your client. In keeping with our example, what aspect of the mortgage process does he or she want you to write about?

Pin them down at the start.

Then, take an important second step. If they say they want an article on, "The best place to get a home mortgage," then simply ask them what *they* think is the best place? When you embrace their ideas in your writing, then you meet their expectations.

You can't be a mind-reader. Ask your client.

You interview your client in a casual, friendly way. He or she should have no idea that you are picking their brain so you can meet their expectations.

Yes, you'll be adding much more content when your research and write, and you'll be turbocharging the article with your creativity. But your client will see their essential thinking in the article and that will please them.

* * *

Let me conclude by saying that, to be successful at content writing, you cannot be vague and general. That's boring. Readers will click away before they get to your third sentence.

You want to take one specific idea and develop it in an interesting way— Interesting enough so it holds reader attention all the way to your call-to-action at the end.

7
GENERAL CONTENT WRITING GUIDE

I'm providing lots of detail, but it's good to pull back and understand your overall objective. That's the point of this chapter. These are guidelines you can use for all types of content writing. I'll be discussing some of these ideas in more detail in a later chapter.

KNOW YOUR AUDIENCE

First, know your audience. This is a trick requirement. Who is your audience? Is it your client or your readers? There's a dilemma for you to consider.

If your client understood his or her audience, there would be no trick to it. But far too many of your clients don't know their audience, so who do you serve? Your client's false expectations or your reader's genuine expectations?

I offer a way around that client problem later, so it's in your best interest, and your client's best interest, if *you* know your reading audience.

Try to discover who they are:

- Men

- Women
- Age group
- Education
- Occupation
- Aspirations

You want to meet the needs of the audience with your writing. Find out as much as you can about your likely readers.

Is there a default parameter for this? Yes. Always think of some pain point your reader may have regarding the topic. Write to ease that pain whatever it may be. Everyone responds in a positive way when you offer solutions to their problems.

There is a place you can get some quick audience insights if your client has a business Facebook page. Your client may not even be aware it exists. If your client grants you access, you can go to his or her business page and click on the "Insights" menu option. Facebook provides a huge amount of helpful information about the company audience there.

That strategy is something you should use with your repeat clients, not casual clients. Also, with repeat clients, you can seek permission to gather audience information via their email list. You can send out a mailing asking what article topics they'd like to see. You can also create polls at places like SurveyMonkey.com to better understand the audience you are trying to reach.

HOOK YOUR READER

You have somewhere around seven seconds to grab the attention of your reader before they click away. You hook them in two ways.

- The first way is with your headline. It needs to be short and enticing. A headline is bait.

- The second part of your hook is your first paragraph. Write something that makes people care. It might be a story, statistic or factoid, but it draws your readers into your content.

Your headline and opening paragraph need a lot of your attention. Sharpen both like a knife.

MAKE IT AN EASY READ

Make reading your content easy on your readers. Get to the point. Famous author Elmore Leonard said, "Leave out the part that readers tend to skip." Funny, but true. Develop strategies to keep people reading.

One way to do that is to write on the level of your audience. Unless you're writing for an academic or other specialized audience, that means you want to write concise sentences at about a 7th or 8th grade level in US schools. That's the understanding level of those who are about 12 to 14 years old.

Most word processors give the Flesch-Kincaid readability score or another measure of reading level. Turn it on, and it will display the reading level of what you have written.

FORMAT FOR READABILITY

As a part of this, keep in mind that the formatting of your content is important. You don't include all these elements in a post in most cases, but you pick the ones that serve your purpose.

People like to read posts with lots of white space, not a wall of type.

- They like sub-heads, one about every 300 words is desirable.
- They like bullet points to summarize key ideas, but not too many.
- Use images and videos.
- Offer charts and graphs if appropriate.
- Add links to sources whenever possible, both to increase reader interest and your own credibility.

Readers will love you when you make your articles visually accessible like this.

BE ENGAGING

There is an overarching principle that I've mentioned before. You must write in an engaging way. Be an interesting writer. Write about thought-provoking things in a stimulating way.

Provide interesting facts and, of course, check those facts. You have an obligation to verify facts from multiple reliable sources. Don't use questionable material or spread hearsay. You may use something controversial to engage readers, and that's okay, but be very clear that it is unsubstantiated.

BE INSPIRING

Content writers must have some passion for what they write. Real passion borne out of their own curiosity and also their desire to help others.

Your ultimate goal as a content writer is to get readers to respond to your call-to-action. You can do that by using all the manipulative tricks in the book, or you can do it with raw passion. I'd like to encourage you to cut loose and motivate others to action by your own passion.

Share both the benefits they'll receive by taking action on the proposition you're presenting. Do it with enthusiasm for their well-being. Paint a picture in the mind of the readers so they can see themselves in a better place by acting on what you have written.

It doesn't cost you anything to be an inspiring writer. It's good to encourage others in positive ways whenever you can.

* * *

These are all important general writing guidelines. They are always in the back of your mind as you write.

- Learn as much as you can about the needs of your readers.

- Make your content easy, interesting to read.

- Hook your reader and draw them through your entire article.

- Inspire your readers to take action.

You want your readers to take action. That's always your goal. It might be an overt action like buying something, or it might be more subtle.

8
A PROVEN WRITING PATTERN

You can't afford the luxury of staring at the screen and wondering what you're going to write about. You know your word count, and you have narrowed your topic, so it's time to start writing.

You're going to be able to write faster and with enhanced quality, if you have a pattern. A template that you follow so you don't have to wonder what you're going to write next.

A COMMON PATTERN

There are many patterns you can use. A common one is:

- Start with a brief story to engage your reader
- Write the body of your content
- Offer a practical application (call-to-action).

One of the benefits of this pattern is that you can repeat it for each major point you're making until you reach your word-length goal.

However, I want to offer you a different pattern that can be far more efficient. Switching the pattern as I outline here has allowed me to research and write a respectable 1,000-word article in an hour or less.

Yes, you must develop your writing muscle over time to adopt this more efficient writing pattern. It's different, but write a dozen articles this way, and you'll probably abandon the traditional "start at the top and work your way down" structure.

AN ADVANCED WRITING PATTERN

There are 10 steps to follow. Don't agonize over each step. You want to move swiftly through most of them.

1. Write down your title and word count. That's your target. You direct your energy towards that. Now do your first of three waves of research.

2. The first wave is to list what you already know about the topic. In some of my books and other writings, I call this "skull diving."

The premise is that you probably already know more than you think about the topic. You're "researching" topic knowledge that's already in your head. Jot down key ideas about what you already know. As you do this, you may realize that there are gaps that raise your curiosity. So, also jot down the questions that pop into your mind.

Or maybe you got key ideas from your client. I talk about client involvement in detail later. In any event, you jot down what you already know. You need to think about the points you're going to cover and make some headers— I suggest three to five— that will be the skeleton of your article. The headings are the natural divisions of your article, the points you intended to cover.

Do you see a pattern in the ideas you've jotted down? There is almost always a logical progression of ideas that emerge early on.

Yes, you can change them later. Right now, you must NARROW and STRUCTURE what you're writing based on what you already know.

3. Do a second wave of research. You have jotted down what you know, so this is the time to discover what you don't know. Be curious, discover interesting things in this second wave of research.

This wave of research will flesh out what you know—you'll probably adjust your outline, your headers to accommodate this new factual information. The real trick is NOT to spend hours doing research. It's easy to get side-tracked. Don't to that— as a content writer, you can't afford it.

Later, I'm going to give you my trick of gathering great research in just a few minutes.

4. If you haven't done it before, break your post into three to five parts. For a 1,000 word article, three points are about right. I gave an example of that in the chapter about narrowing your topic.

You have been playing with this in your first and second wave of research, but this is the time to set your final structure. Know what goes under each of those three headings at this point.

5. This is going to seem strange. Before you start writing your three points under those headers, write your conclusion (call-to-action) first.

Weird, I know, but try it and you'll like it. The trip goes faster when you know your destination.

> *The whole point of content writing is to inform and persuade in the most entertaining way possible. Your purpose is to sell products, services or ideas to site visitors in the most positive and inspiring way you can. Have that purpose fixed in your mind before you start writing.*

So, write the conclusion first. Then shape your introduction and your three (or more) points to dovetail into the conclusion you are writing first.

Some people think that writing an article is like writing a "seat of the pants" novel. Those writers don't know how it's going to turn out. Well, as a content writer, you want to know.

Once you have your title and have done your first two waves of research, you know the outcome you're seeking. That's why you write it now, at this stage, before you write anything else.

6. You're now ready to write the heart of the article. That's the three to five points you researched. The headers as the bones. Use your research to hang the meat on those bones.

Write everything you know and have learned about the topic. Don't self-edit—let the information gush from your brain to the page. This is *not* the time to stop and ponder the meaning of the universe, whether your life has meaning and purpose, or even if what you're writing makes sense. This is your first draft. Right now, you simply want to get words on the page without second-guessing yourself. Don't stop writing for any reason. Save your revisions for later.

7. You will likely have a few holes in your article. You wanted to include a quote, statistic or fact but skipped over it because you didn't stop writing for any reason.

Now is the time to do some quick research to fill in the blanks. This is the third wave of your research.

Remember, when you're writing, you just write. You don't do additional research or editing until it's all down on the page. Think first, then write. Stopping to think while you are writing is going to cost you time and money.

8. Almost there. You need an introduction. A hook to grab reader interest. Now is the time to write it.

You write the introduction last because you have written everything else at this point. You have all the information and insight you need to write a snappy and captivating hook.

If you have a story or statistic, use that. You get those in wave one or two of your research, so you should have it saved and ready to use. Don't have a story or statistic? Rephrase your conclusion. Putting it in the form of a question often works well to grab reader interest.

9. Revise your article. If you have done it right, you have used the creative right side of your brain to let your article gush from your brain based on your research. At this point, you want to put your logical left brain to work. Examine the logic of what you have written. Check the flow. Think about your reader—have you attracted and retained their interest? Now is the time to revise what you have written and put it into final form.

10. Copy edit your work. Copy editing is checking your grammar, spelling, and punctuation. I have dedicated a chapter to editing, and it comes up later.

I've said it before because it is so important to write with speed and quality. Don't write and edit at the same time. That's a major time-waster. Write—don't stop for any reason—and edit after you finished your first complete draft.

* * *

What is the benefit of writing in this pattern? You can write a credible article, one with substance, and most importantly, you can do it quickly. Here are the six key movements of your symphony:

- Capture ideas by doing research

- Structure what you discovered

- Write quickly without inhibition

- Revise your work to fix flow and facts

- Edit—Check grammar, spelling, and punctuation

- Be happy

Quality and speed—that's how you make money as a content writer.

9
HOW TO DO FAST RESEARCH

Your ability to write content at a moneymaking pace is largely dictated by your ability to research topics quickly. In this chapter, I'm going to share a few research tips and tricks.

LIMIT YOUR GEOGRAPHY

I'm going to suggest that you confine your research to the room where you write. In almost all cases you don't want to travel during your research and writing tie, even to the local Starbucks for a cup of coffee. That takes time, and in most cases, you're not getting paid enough to do that.

You even want to avoid going to your local city or university library. Again—that's time-consuming. You want to do as much research as you can from the room where you work.

USE THE CORRECT SEARCH ENGINE

Use Google sparingly. Is that shocking to you? Most people go to Google to find answers to questions. That's mostly the wrong place to go for a professional writer. A traditional search engine like Google returns a list of results sorted in accordance with its search algorithm. In order to get results you can use, you must choose your search terms carefully. In fact, you may have to use many different terms to find something that's useful.

And again, Google is designed to show you the most popular information, not the information that may be the most helpful to you as a content writer. Generally speaking, you don't want to write about the same old stuff that anyone can already find on Google. You want to provide unique, interesting information that helps people solve the problems they face. These are not mutually exclusive in all cases, but you want to dig deeper for online information, rather than continue in the Google rut.

When it comes to seeing what information is available for a particular topic, and to find material that is not held hostage to Google's search algorithm, you need to use both a Cluster search engine and specialized search engines.

CLUSTER SEARCH ENGINES

A Cluster search engine organizes data differently than Google. With Google, you must input precise, highly refined search terms to get the results you want. Then, they are displayed in a long list of "14,234,356" results. Most people look no further than the first page of results, Researchers are inclined to go deeper—like page 5 (50 results), but after that, the gold turns to brass in most cases. Google is a popular but so-so data mining tool. It exists primarily to sell advertising.

A Cluster search engine turns Google on its head. You can input a general term and get specific results. And these results are organized by topics and categories, so it is easy to look at many different aspects of any topic.

There are several research sites that you can use, but I'm a big fan of iSeek.com (also available at iSeek.ai), which, at this writing is free to use. Why is it great? I suggest you go to that site and play around with it and see the amazing results you can get, and how it will speed your content writing research.

Notice some special features of iSeek and why I like it so much.

- You can search the web in general. This is more like a Google search for general information, except the data is sorted by topics and categories.

- Are you researching a medical or health-related topic? Input your term and click on the medical icon before you search. In this case, you'll not only get clustered results, but you'll get them from specialized health sources. I discuss specialized search engines next.

- You have the same Cluster/specialized options for education. I like to use the education option because of the diverse kinds of information you can see. I typed in the word, "Texas Statehood" (a very general term), and I got access to 7,783 web pages, 586 videos, 313 books, 45 files, 34 documents, and 11 slide presentations. Other searches also show audio and images. That's right, all from just typing two words into the iSeek search box.

- Finance is another specialize option offered by iSeek. Earlier, I used the example of "The Best Place to Get a Home Mortgage" as a way of drilling down on a topic. In iSeek, I used that term in their finance option, and that resulted in 380 results in eight different categories. In addition, the search provided 280 news sources and 50 social media links.

Are there other Cluster search engines? There used to be a number of them, but they have been gobbled up by corporations and fees to use them are high. There are only two free Cluster search engines I would recommend, iSeek and Carrot (Carrot2.org), which is an open source project.

SPECIALIZED SEARCH ENGINES

Many people don't realize that there are other types of specialized search engines. If you're a professional content writer, you want to use them at every opportunity.

Google Scholar is an example of a specialized search engine. This part of the Google search interface searches professional journals of all kinds—all fields of knowledge including art, business, medicine, science—you name it.

Most scholarly journals charge big dollars to read the full article, but their free abstracts usually supply enough information for an online blog post or article. The abstracts usually discuss the method and the conclusions of the research, and that's what most of your readers will want to know.

Google Scholar a great place to ferret out facts that will add substance and quality to many kinds of blog posts or articles. Generally, you want to digest and simplify the things you find there. Your goal is to help your readers understand often complex topics.

You don't have to rely on Google Scholar. You can get credible research fast from other places. These search engines offer a gateway into some of them.

- BASE -Bielefeld Academic Search Engine. Base-Search.net

- Refseek.com. Offers specialized results, but also has a "document" option so you can dive deeper with PDF documents and reports.

- ResearchGate.net. Biotech, drug development, life sciences.

Make no mistake, there are a large number of specialized search engines that deal with particular topics. You need to develop your own list of the ones you find most useful.

Some writers go to Wikipedia, but not professionals. Doing research there is like eating your meals out of a dumpster. Have some self-respect as a writing professional and avoid Wikipedia. If you do go there, forget the article and look at the references at the bottom. Visit and quote the references, but never quote Wikipedia as a source.

FAST OFFLINE RESEARCH

Where can you get unique, credible and usually quick information? Don't rely on searches; talk to a real person. You might know an expert on the topic you're writing about. Send them an email, call them or do a video Skype interview.

If you don't know an expert personally, find one. Where do you find an expert? It depends on the topic. You can often find one in your area by calling around and getting referrals. If the topic is a complex one, use one of these resources:

- ExpertiseFinder.com
- JournalistsResource.org
- FindAnExpertOnline.com

There are also many specialized professional organizations that can refer you to an expert in a particular field. Universities are another tremendous source of experts to interview.

Most experts will be happy to talk to you free, especially those in your community. However, some high-profile experts may charge a fee, and you'll want to know about that before you start the interview.

Two quick points. First, always be polite when you talk to experts. Their time is valuable. Usually, you contact them by email in advance and see if they will talk to you, and then set a time to do it.

Before the interview, write out no more than 3-4 questions to ask them. That's probably all you'll need for a 1,000-word article. Keep in mind you are not engaging them in a free-wheeling conversation. You're seeking specific information about a topic.

Respect professional boundaries. Be sure the person knows that you'll be quoting them in the article and get their permission for that.

The second point—in many places it is illegal to record a conversation without getting explicit permission first. This requires a second level of permission. The first is to use the content, the second is to record their voice or image.

Ask for permission before you record, then start recording and ask again so you have a record of getting permission. You want to get explicit permission all the time, but especially if you're recording a phone or Skype conversation.

* * *

In conclusion, you want to do your research as quickly as possible. You want to use the best, most credible sources possible.

- Speed up the process by using a Cluster search engine.

- Stay away from junk information sites. High-class junk like Wikipedia or low-class junk sites filled with extremism or conspiracy theories.

- Interview people whenever you can. It's a quick way to get fresh, authoritative content.

Remember that you're doing research in three waves. You can see my advanced writing pattern system to refresh your mind about the process.

10
HOW TO BE AN ORIGINAL WRITER

You don't want to steal the work of other people, on purpose or by accident, either by copyright infringement or by plagiarism. But how do you do research, collect ideas and make your content unique? That is an important question for all content writers.

If you're a writer, you're probably like other creative people and me and hate it when people steal from you. So, it's good to know the legal and ethical boundaries.

A RANT ABOUT INTELLECTUAL PROPERTY RIGHTS

Please excuse a little rant from me. It's an issue to me when people steal intellectual property, something protected by the law of all nations, yet don't see themselves as evildoers. I hope it becomes an issue to you too.

These morally corrupt people think they are justified in being thieves. But stealing intellectual property such is online articles, books, music, film and online courses is no different than robbing a store or a bank.

Being a thief is a moral defect. It's about the character of the person doing the stealing. It really doesn't make any difference what they're stealing or why— it's a mark of a flawed personality.

Same goes for those who use anything that might be stolen. They have their own kind of moral corruption.

You don't agree with me? That's okay. As a writer, you will be creating different kinds of intellectual property, whether it be articles, books, film scripts, courses, or whatever. Someday someone will steal from you, and then you will sing a different song. You'll realize they are talking food off your table.

Some creatives say the thieves wouldn't pay for your content anyway, so there is no income loss. Some say theft is a form of marketing and is okay. Both are nonsense. Car dealership owners don't say, "Steal cars off my lot; it's good advertising." Bankers don't say "Steal our money—we'll get more depositors if you do."

If you want to make money, take a firm stand against people who are soft on intellectual property crime. They are stealing from you.

Okay, my rant is over. But it's one that I hope you'll remember it.

CONTENT CREATORS AND FAIR USE

Now, let's turn our attention to ourselves as content creators. We gather material from sources all the time, so how do you keep away from copyright infringement. How do you avoid plagiarism?

Copyright is a way of protecting intellectual property so the person who creates it can get an income from their work. Only the creator of the work is able to grant the right to others to make copies — thus, the term copyright.

You can avoid copyright infringement in most cases by simply putting the words you use in quotes and attributing the quote to the author and source. It's as simple as that.

If you use longer quotes, then you need to get written permission from the content creator. Sometimes there's a fee attached to getting that permission. Giving credit to the author is not the same as getting permission.

Lots of writers have heard of the "Fair Use" provisions of the US Copyright law. They think they can use anything in any way they wish, but that's totally wrong. The Fair Use law has very strict requirements, and you must abide by them.[10]

In any event, the Fair Use laws don't give you permission to use copyrighted material. Fair Use is just a possible defense you can use in court after someone sues you. Ignorance is no excuse when it comes to violating copyright laws.

THE PERILS OF PLAGIARISM

There is another kind of intellectual property theft called plagiarism. That's when a person changes the words of others and then claims it as their own work.

However, plagiarism is more complex than it seems. All writers are inspired by the ideas of others, so what are the boundaries?

Plagiarism is not a crime in the United States, but it is closely related to copyright infringement. People often pay huge fines and suffer great humiliation for rearranging the words of others and then claiming them as their own.

There is a kind of software called "article spinners." They take an article and allegedly change the text just enough to make it seem different. But it's not really different. No fresh, unique ideas are added. They are really just plagiarism machines, I'd say.

ORIGINAL IDEAS MAY NOT EXIST

There are some problems with the concept of plagiarism. The first was pointed out by raconteur Wilson Mizner. He remarked, "If you steal from one author it's plagiarism; if you steal from many it's research."

The simple fact is, we are all standing on the shoulders of those who have gone before us. There is no question that humanity is in the constant process of reshaping existing ideas. It's not wrong. The entire issue is *how* you recycle those ideas.

The academic world is a stickler about getting "original thinking" in the papers that students write. But they are often hypocritical. After all, the things they are teaching in universities are not original in almost all cases. They are just recycling the knowledge of the ages. Individual professors recycle their lectures from year-to-year and seldom cite their sources except in vague ways.

Plus, from the kind of disruptions we have been seeing on campus in recent years, original thinking seems to be a thing of the past. Students are required to conform to the ideas of the herd.

An ancient teacher said, "What has been will be again, what has been done will be done again; there is nothing new under the sun."[11] That should be the starting point of the thought process, not robotically trying to identify the similarity of words and phrases. "Originality" has always been a matter of thinking about old ideas in new ways.

THERE IS A PROFIT-MAKING PLAGIARISM DETECTION INDUSTRY

Another problem with plagiarism is that a profit-making industry has grown up around it. The Internet allows "string searches," and that means these companies have the power to compare what you have written with what everyone else in the world has written and is available. If sentences match, then you have deemed a plagiarist. That's not always true, of course, but that's their assumption.

Sadly, this moneymaking scheme is aided and abetted by the academic community. They use this technology to accuse students of plagiarism, real or imagined.

These plagiarism detection companies have either started websites or support existing ones, to redefine plagiarism in ways that scare people into buying their services.

For example, Plagiarism.org seeks to portray itself as an authority site to enrich human knowledge. Who owns it and is now using it to redefine plagiarism? TurnItIn LLC, who bill themselves as, "World's No.1 Plagiarism Checker"[12] They have redefined plagiarism to make it more onerous than it is, then want to sell a tool to unmask it. This is a self-serving arrangement that seems highly unethical to some people.

SOCIAL STANDING MAY CHANGE THE SERIOUSNESS OF PLAGIARISM

If you are a student, expect a serious whack from your professor if you violate the plagiarism policy in place. They may even want to throw you out of school. But if you are in ideological harmony with the institution, show promise, or have social position, they may wink at it. They will go out of their way to make excuses for you about your plagiarism.

As an example of this, let's look at Joseph Biden, who served 36 years as a US Senator and two-terms as Vice-President of the United States. My comments are not politically motivated in any sense but do demonstrate how people are not treated equally when it comes to plagiarism.

Biden graduated from the University of Delaware and presumably he learned how to write papers there. Most people learn that skill and its protocols on that level. However, when he reached Syracuse University College of Law, he was accused of plagiarism. Did he clip a sentence here and there and call it his own? No, his paper was 15 pages, and he stole 5 pages of it from a law review article. However, Biden was personable, had potential, and only failed the course for his wrong-doing and was not kicked out of law school.[13]

How did Biden later characterize his blatant plagiarism? He called it a mistake of his youth (he was 25 and married), and he said his cheating was not "malevolent," whatever that means. He told a reporter that he had simply misunderstood the need to cite sources carefully.[14]

Why did Biden's student plagiarism become an issue in 1987? He was running for the presidency himself at the time, and it was discovered that he was actively plagiarizing John F. Kennedy, Hubert H. Humphrey, and British politician Neil Kinnock.[15] Reports of his serial plagiarism forced him out of the campaign at that point, but in 2008 Barrack Obama picked Biden as his running mate.

Political privilege extended to Barrack Obama too. In a video[16], he is seen clearly plagiarizing the exact words of fellow-Democrat John Edwards and later copying the words, without attribution, of his friend Deval Patrick. Regardless of what side of the political aisle you're on, it's shocking when pundits make lame excuses for plagiarism as happens so often.[17]

One of America's most revered contemporary social leaders was a plagiarist. The Rev. Dr. Martin Luther King, Jr. copied words from others, without attribution, claimed them as his own, and included them in his doctoral dissertation at Boston University. A special Boston University committee reported:

> There is no question but that Dr. King plagiarized in the dissertation by appropriating material from sources not explicitly credited in notes, or mistakenly credited, or credited generally and at some distance in the text from a close paraphrase or verbatim quotation.[18]

Normally, a university would revoke the doctoral degree if the person took credit for the words of others as if they were his own. That is the most basic kind of plagiarism. However, Boston University did not do that. They said, "no thought should be given to the revocation of Dr. King's doctoral degree" because, they indicated, it would serve no purpose,[19] not even, apparently, as a deterrent to other would-be plagiarists. They ended up putting a note about the plagiarism in the university library copy of Dr. King's dissertation.

We know that plagiarism is not a crime. However, copyright infringement can be prosecuted in civil court and sometimes in criminal court. But, as we have seen, plagiarism is not the "burn in hell" offense as characterized by the plagiarism detection industry and their academic co-conspirators.

How should we characterize plagiarism? It is merely a social taboo. It shows sloppy thinking, a lack of respect for other thinkers and writers, and a lack of skill in putting a document together. We see that sort of thing in all aspects of life. Writing is little different than designing and building a car, website or anything else. We are all working off each other's ideas, so uniqueness is in the details.

Plagiarism is like pornography— you know it when you see it. But there is no shame in recycling the ideas of others. Just do it well.

Profit-making "Plagiarism detection" corporations, in collusion with the academic community, are victimizing writers, in my opinion. They are both busy making rules and assigning culpability, but they are not teaching students how to think. They will gladly tell them what to think, but not how to think. People who know how to think don't worry about plagiarism. Most of their thoughts don't require attribution, but if they do, they are always happy to give credit where credit is due.

MEET KIRBY FERGUSON

Kirby Ferguson has a great perspective, and content writers can learn from him. He has several TED Talks, and in each one he repeats an important mantra: "Copy, Transform, Combine." That's what all great artists and authors have done, and that's what content writers also do. He says nothing is original; we only add our own perspectives to old ideas to give them contemporary meaning.

Many people copy and stop there. They are intellectually crippled and have no moral compass. However, truly creative people are able to absorb their world, copy it into their brain where they transform it and combine it with other knowledge and experience to create something innovative. That is the heart of what Kirby Ferguson teaches. As he defines it, "Remix is to combine or edit existing materials to produce something new." He says that this is the basic element of creativity.[20]

That's what you want to do as you create content. Use the ideas of many to create a unique perspective that grabs your readers.

Kirby Ferguson shows examples of people like Henry Ford, Bob Dylan, Steve Jobs and others who have taken existing ideas and reshaped them into something unique. The video[21] is illuminating and will give you some insight about your role as a writer.

Ferguson talks about the four steps to getting an idea,[22] and he is not the first one to come up with them. I have discussed them earlier in a different context, out of my own experience, not his. However, what he has to say is a summary of an age-old process. To get an idea, he says:

- Create boundaries.

    This is similar to what I have said about content writers narrowing a topic before you research and write.

- Consume (learn about) everything within the boundary.

    This is the research we do.

- Study the materials and organize them.

    This is structuring the article as I have discussed.

- Drop it.

    Ferguson says to let the idea percolate before advancing with it. This is not a bad suggestion, but most content writers have deadlines to meet, so we cannot lavish too much percolation time on an idea.

The percolation time is really reshaping time. This is when content writers reshape what they have learned into something fresh. It is not a matter of copying what we have learned, but it is much like recycling, where a wrecked car is compressed, melted down and transformed into another car by a different automaker.

Philosopher Simone Weil said, "The future is made of the same stuff as the present." The present is made of the same stuff as the past, too. As content writers, we want to respect the intellectual property rights of others, but we need to realize they were recycling ideas too.

* * *

All creative people have a little cup and dip it into a great river of existing ideas. You are not stealing their work or their ideas if you remix and recycle them in a unique way.

I have used the word "unique" many times in this book. Uniqueness is what keeps you out of trouble when it comes to copyright laws and plagiarism allegations.

And that's the heart of it. You must process ideas in your brain and make them your own. Add your education and experience to your varied research. Reshape the material into something unique and fresh to meet the needs of today's readers.

11
HOW TO BE INTERESTING

Your goal is to write content that people want to read. I talked about some of these ideas in a general way in a different context in an earlier chapter, but here we are seeing how these elements of writing and presentation can help you hold reader attention. That translates into making you a more interesting writer.

Being interesting is an important part of your mission as a content writer. If you're able to capture reader interest and get them to respond to your call-to-action, then you will have a golden future.

You see, everyone wants results. The reader wants to learn something helpful. The person hiring you wants to sell products, services or an idea. You want a steady flow of work from happy clients. When you write in a way that achieves results, you become a very popular person. Being an interesting writer and being an effective writer go hand-in-hand.

CAPTURE READER INTEREST QUICKLY

If you don't capture reader interest, all your work is in vain. You can grab the attention of potential readers in these ways:

1. The title of the article. People are attracted by certain words in the title, and you want to use them. There are resources to find these words but let me give you an idea of what I mean.

- One of the top attention grabbers in an article is the phrase "how to." People constantly want to know how to do something. You'll grab attention if you entitle your article, "How to Fix a Coffee Maker," or "How to do Brain Surgery at Home." The article might not be a how-to article. However, if you can somehow plausibly use the phrase "how-to" in your title, then you should do it.

- Another attention grabber is using numbers in your title. "Five Ways to Fix Your Coffee Maker" or "Five Ways to do Brain Surgery at Home."

- Another attractive word to use in your title — Why. "Why You Should Fix Your Own Coffee Maker" or "Why You Should Do Brain Surgery at Home."

Do you get the idea? These special words intrigue potential readers. These are only examples, and there are many other trigger words you can and should use.[23]

2. Your first paragraph must be short, sweet and intriguing. Think of your readers as fish sniffing around your title, which is a hook. But they want to know if what you have to say is good enough to eat. Therefore, your first sentence means everything. It needs to set the hook.

I have mentioned elsewhere what needs to go in your short introduction. You want to set the hook with as few words and sentences as possible. Generally, a statistic, amazing factoid, shocking quote, or the start of a captivating story does the job.

Stories are the most difficult, but they can be the most appealing. You need a first sentence that sucks people into the story, even though the story might end up being three or more precise paragraphs long.

This is an essential thought — the purpose of your introduction is to set the hook in your reader. You'll sell them the product, service or idea later, but your first goal is to get them reading. They will not read your informative or persuasive content until you get the hook into them.

3. Put ideas together in creative ways. Even if you're writing about a fascinating topic, it's possible to present it in a boring and lackluster way. You don't want to do that.

To add spark to your prose, convey the material in simple words, short sentences, and relatively short paragraphs.

No matter what you're writing about, you must develop the idea in a logical way. People demand a logical progression in everything they read.

4. Present your content in a visually inviting way. You can do this in several ways.

- Use headers and sub-headers to break content up into bite-sized portions. Make them as enticing as your title. Usually, you do not want more than about 300 words under each header. This keeps readers interested. It also helps with search engine optimization, SEO, which I talk about in detail in chapter 12.

- Use images if feasible. These might include pictures or charts and graphs. Ask your client if he or she has images. Be sure to charge extra if your client wants you to acquire or create them.

- Use bullet points to break out key thoughts under headers. You can see how effective that can be in this section.

Website content readers are scanners, and you keep their interest with bullet points. You never want to be guilty of presenting your readers with a "wall of type."

BE A CURIOUS CAT

In my view, the best way to be an interesting writer is to be a curious cat and to share your infectious curiosity with your readers. Nothing attracts and hold attention better than the enthusiasm with which you share what you have learned with readers.

That will pose a conundrum for some writers. Why? Because it is sometimes difficult to be enthusiastic about all the writing assignments you receive. That's something you need to think about as you accept assignments. As a professional writer, you should be able to write about any topic. On the other hand, you may want to initially limit the range of topics that you are happy to write about.

My advice is that you sit down in advance and make a list of topics that interest you. You may not have full knowledge of them, but you should be interested enough to be willing to research them.

With that perspective, you can have many different topics on your list, from health care to parenting to real estate—actually thousands of different topics. But you can keep nuclear physics off your list if you can't write about it enthusiastically.

> *Don't limit yourself too much. Remember, curiosity does not kill cats. Curiosity lines the pockets of content writers. Content writers are on an endless voyage of discovery and research is their catnip.*

There is no question that eventually a client will come to you with a job for a topic you never considered. That's okay. Think about what you already know about the topic and combine them with your curiosity quotient. Take the job, no matter what the topic may be if you think you're up to it.

ONE TOPIC, EXCLUDE OTHERS?

Many writers are particularly enthusiastic about one topic. They are experts in it and like to share their knowledge about it.

It's good to be an expert on a topic. It's great to be a well-known, "go-to" person in a particular field. I know people who have made serious money by specializing in content about a single topic. Like online marketing OR engineering OR health care OR the pharmaceutical industries. Not all these topics, they are an expert in only one.

If people recognize you as an expert in a certain field, they will be willing to pay you premium prices for your writing on that topic. As I discuss in the pricing chapter, you want to get premium prices for your work whenever possible.

It's a good idea to develop a specialty. The big question is whether or not there is enough demand in that field to keep you busy. Sometimes people become very successful in a narrow writing niche. It's a good thing when it happens. The problem is, it doesn't happen that often.

THE BEST PLAN

What's the best plan? In my view, it is better to start out as a generalist taking on all the topics that you feel you want to write about. As you do that over the months and years, develop a specialty for which you can command premium prices.

But don't give up writing on a variety of topics. That work will provide you with regular paydays, and those rare premium specialty writing jobs will add a welcome boost to your income.

Is it true that you might be able to move away from the more ordinary type of content writing, and do nothing but jobs in your specialty? Yes, it is possible if you find a lucrative niche and work at developing it.

* * *

You have an obligation to be an interesting writer. The best way to do that is by getting the attention of potential readers with a captivating headline and then setting the hook with a great first sentence or paragraph.

You keep their interest by drawing them through each section with enticing headers and sub-headers. The visual presentation of your content is also important to keep people reading.

What you write and how you write it is essential, of course. But even the best-written content can seem boring if you do not infuse it with your enthusiasm.

12
BE SEO AWARE

Gadzooks! You're a writer, but here we are talking about Search Engine Optimization. That's what SEO stands for. It's important because your client's target audience needs to find your article before they can read it.

After they read it, and respond to your call-to-action, then you have a happy client that will come back and want to pay you repeatedly for your expertise.

HOW SEO WORKS

How does SEO help people find the article you have written? Well, you may think what I'm about to say is fake, but it's not.

You see, search engines like Google are dumb. That seems incomprehensible since you can be looking on Amazon for a camera, and the next website you visit — like Facebook or a news site — you see an Amazon ad for the exact same camera you were looking at the short time before.

From that, we would gather that search engines are smart. But they're not. They are dumber than a bag of hammers.

They search pages on a website and index what they find, but they are so dumb you must repeat certain keywords that describe what your article is about so the search "spider" will know what it's looking at. That repetition is one of the main ways search engines know what your article is about.

MIND-READING REQUIRED

Seems strange but simple enough, doesn't it? But there's more.

The keywords you repeatedly include in your article must be the words people type into the search box for articles dealing with the topic that you have written about.

So that means you need to be clairvoyant. You must be able to predict what people will type into the Google search box so Google can match that search with the keywords in your article.

Well, maybe I was going overboard a bit when I said you must be clairvoyant. The best way to get keywords to include in your article is to ask your client which keywords they want to use.

The other best way is to use SEO tools[24] to see discover likely key words you can use based on what people have already been using.

Here's something very important— no one types in a single keyword and expects to get results. So the term keyword is a misnomer. People can't find anything really helpful by typing a single keyword in the search box. They type in keyword phrases.

If I type in the word "Hammer," I get nearly 95 million results, and the top one is about a museum.

If I type in a keyword phrase like, "Bag of hammers," I get completely different results. If I search for "dumb as a bag of hammers," I get a definition of the phrase.

So you want to use keyword PHRASES that puts your article near the top of the first page on a Google search. There's a lot of competition for that real estate, but that's the name of the SEO game.

It takes lots of research time to find the best keyword phrases, so you can't afford to spend time doing that without pay.

If your client wants you to do the research to supply the keyword phrases you include in your text, then you want to charge them extra. I discuss this in a later chapter. I can guarantee you that you can't make any money writing articles if you're doing keyword research without pay.

Now, I can't go into all the details about how to do keyword research. That's why I entitled this chapter, "Be SEO Aware." I want to make you aware that you need to include keyword phrases in your article, even though SEO is a huge field of study in its own right.

HOW TO BUILD SEO INTO YOUR CONTENT

Here are a few helpful tips about including keywords in your document. Here they are:

- List the keywords/phrases you intend to target before you start to write.
- Try to include the keyword phrase in the title.
- Make an effort to include the keyword phrase in the first sentence.

- See if you can include the keyword phrase in at least one header.

- Use the keyword phrase once or twice in your body copy, or a few extra times, if you do not include it in the title or header.

You can't insert these phrases just anywhere. Real people will be reading your writing, so you must use as much finesse as possible to integrate them properly in context.

It's more important to write for people than it is with the machine that will be searching for your document, but you must do both.

Here's an important issue — you can't use a keyword phrase too often or Google will penalize you. It's called "keyword spamming." You don't want to do that. Your keyword phrases should not exceed more than about 3% or 4% of your total word count.

* * *

The more you know about SEO the better. It's essential for blog posts and can be important for other types of content writing.

Try to get your client to give you the keyword phrases they want you to use before you start the job. Then, you must use your best writing skills to integrate them in the ways I described. You don't want your keywords to be intrusive to your readers.

If your client is unwilling to pay you to do keyword phrase research, then you must leave them out of your document. Clients are unrealistic and unfair when they pay you a fee to write, but expect you to do extensive keyword phrase research for nothing.

There are other aspects of SEO that are outside the purview of this book but are important, like linking and getting backlinks. SEO is a specialty.

So, learn as much about SEO as you can. Use keyword phrases as effectively as you can. That is an important key to content writing success.

13
REVISION AND EDITING

There is a distinction between revising your writing and editing it. No matter what you're writing — web content or a book — the first draft is just the first step of the writing process. Your revisions may take you into second, third or fourth drafts. Well, with books anyway. Short articles usually require one draft and one revision before you edit it and send it to your client. Your client may request another revision, and that will require a final edit.

What are revisions? That's when you go over your draft and make sure you have said what you intended to say in the way you intended to say it.

What is editing? In the strictest sense, it is what is known as copy editing, and that's the process where you check grammar, spelling, and punctuation.

Revision and copy editing are not done at the same time. You only want to edit your best and final revision.

STEPS IN THE PROCESS

A first draft enables you to get your ideas down. You are able to see the structure and flow and make decisions about how to improve it in the second draft. You may add new content or delete sentences or paragraphs you have written. You may shift paragraphs around. You may tighten up your introduction to grab attention better and tweak the call-to-action to make it more compelling.

All of this is called revision. You are still working creatively on the right side of your brain. When you are satisfied with ,the content and how it is structured via the revision phases, then you move to the logical left side of your brain to do copy editing.

The second draft is usually good enough to send to your client. But before you do that, you must copy edit your final draft. Online content is generally quick and easy to edit, but it's something you must do. You are checking grammar, spelling, and punctuation to make sure it is of professional quality.

If you followed the writing pattern that I suggested in an earlier chapter, you should have a well-structured and well-written article.

COPY EDITING PROCEDURE

Professional writers don't write and edit at the same time. Some say they can do both simultaneously, but I always make a funny snorting sound when I hear someone say that. It's that humorous. It doesn't work. It will slow you down.

- The first step in the copy editing process is to let your final draft settle for at least an hour or two, longer if possible. Grab lunch and then come back to it.

- The second step is to read what you have written. Don't read it silently. Read it out loud. That's essential. Is the title good?

Does your introduction grab interest? Have you grouped interesting content under eye-catching headers? Does what you have written makes sense? Anything you need to add? Anything you should delete?

- Your third step is to scrutinize every sentence. Are all words spelled correctly? Is the capitalization and punctuation as it should be? Have you used acronyms consistently? Have you eliminated all those pesky adverbs and exclamation points?

See — three easy steps, and you have cleaned up your article, and it probably approaches a professional level. At least you have rid it of the embarrassing things that your client or readers might catch.

I edit nearly a dozen books per year or clients, most of whom I had for many years. Book editing goes far deeper. But what I have outlined above is a simple professional approach for online articles.

Revising and editing can be that easy. Just keep in mind that they are two separate functions. But let me add just a few things to take it to a higher level.

THE NEXT LEVEL

To take you to a higher level in article editing, I want to suggest that you avoid depending on the built-in Microsoft Word spelling and grammar checker.

Yes, by all means, use both. But don't become overly dependent upon them. They usually catch only the most egregious errors, and many smaller problems slip through.

I also want to advise you against using a tool like Grammarly to do your editing. I have used it in the past, and I believe it causes more problems than it solves. There's a free version, but I think it's pretty useless since it excludes 150 editing issues that most people would expect to have. You can buy a subscription, but in my opinion, it is vastly overpriced.

One of the biggest faults with Grammarly is that way it presents errors; you need to be a grammar expert to correct them. That's counterproductive to my way of thinking.

There are simple tools like the Hemingway Editor[25] that can help you edit your articles. It performs basic functions like showing word count, reading level, over-use of adverbs, instances of passive voice, and it highlights overly long or convoluted sentences.

Hemingway Editor is basic. I think it has a place, however, because it presents your content in a new light. It causes you to look closer at what you have written. You will see issues that you missed because you wrote the material and are probably too familiar with it.

ULTIMATE EDITING

What is the ultimate way to make sure your work is properly edited? Hire a professional copy editor. No, not your mom or a former teacher, but someone who is aware of contemporary (last five or so years) editing practices. You don't want a proofreader, who corrects proofs and should never edit anything. You want an experienced copy editor. Professionals know the difference between the two jobs and don't claim to do both.

There is a two-fold problem with hiring a professional. One is the cost, which you will have to pay. The other is scheduling. You are trying to make money with quick turnarounds, and waiting a week or two for the editor to get to your job is usually not feasible.

What is the best course of action? My suggestion is that you become familiar with the rules and edit your own articles. If you need to brush up on grammar, visit the Purdue University Online Writing Lab (OWL).[26]

No matter what you write, you want to follow a particular style guide. When you do that, you eliminate a lot of guesswork about what gets capitalized, if numbers should be spelled out, or if book names get quotation marks or are italicized, and that sort of thing.

Different style books have different ways of addressing these details. I strongly suggest you get the latest edition of the *Associated Press (AP) Stylebook*. It has fresh, contemporary conventions used by the news media rather than the stodgy academic style that you see in the *Chicago Manual of Style* and other such guides.

CLIENT REVISIONS

In my early days of content writing, I worked cheap. I regret that, but I learned something very important about doing client revisions.

I'm going to impart my hard-earned knowledge about doing client revisions with you now. There is a distinction between the revisions you do as a writer and client revisions. When you do revisions, you are refining your work. Client revisions are different. A client has found things he or she doesn't like in your finished article and wants you to change them.

The first thing to know is that client revisions are a necessary evil. You will finish your document, the client will read it, and sometimes he or she will want you to revise all or part of it. That goes with the territory.

Doing revisions to keep a client happy is good business. But that comes with some caveats, which I'm highlighting here.

HAVE A BUSINESSLIKE RELATIONSHIP

The first lesson I learned is that if you work cheap, your client will not respect you. You must project yourself as an expert with lots of experience, then prove it with quality writing.

The sad reality is, most clients don't know good writing from bad—they just think they do. Therefore, you should have an advantage.

The worst clients want you to work cheap. They want you to research the topic, write, do keyword research and endless revisions for a few cents a word. That will make you go crazy. And then, they will ask you to do endless changes with no regard for your time.

You want to do revisions when needed, but you want to avoid a master-slave relationship with an overly-picky client. My policy is to make frivolous changes, but then never work for the client again. Good clients will value your expert skill and will pay you accordingly.

PLAN AHEAD TO MINIMIZE REVISIONS

How do you minimize revisions? There are two main things you can do:

1. Have a clear understanding with your client about the topic in advance. Get a working title from your client and keyword phrases they want to be included. If your client shares these things with you over the phone, immediately send an email confirming the details of the conversation, so you have them in writing.

2. Do a brief interview and ask your client what he or she thinks is the most important aspects of the topic. They have their opinions, and they'll be looking for them to be expressed in your final document.

They'll ask you to revise your document if they don't find those opinions. So, don't try to read their mind. Ask them what they think is most important about the topic and then you can do research to enrich your writing.

My main point is a simple one. A certain amount of client revisions is a necessary evil. You want to do as few of them as needed. You can eliminate the number of revisions you need to do if you have a clear understanding of the project at the beginning.

In my experience, I have found that it never pays to debate the revision suggestions a client makes. I might say something like, "I wouldn't do that for several reasons, but it's your call."

They are paying, so I just let them live under the illusion that their suggestions have merit. Actually, once in a while they do have merit, but less often than you'd think.

On the other hand, I have developed relationships with clients over many years, and they paid me well, not only for my writing but also for my judgment. I am happy to give advice to these kinds of well-paying clients. They usually take my advice, but it's no problem for me when they don't.

So—establish your authority as a writer, plan ahead, determine expectations in advance and write well. That is the clear path to fewer revisions.

* * *

You see, there is a cycle of writing online content. The title, the word count, the outline, the phases of research, the writing, the revision, and the copy editing.

But don't think of this like the slow-rolling cycle of the seasons. Think of it as the cycle of a washing machine. Wash, spin dry, rinse and repeat.

You should be able to go through the article creation cycle as quickly as your washing machine goes through a wash cycle. You are not a machine, but you can develop your skills to work efficiently.

: PART THREE :
BUILDING YOUR BUSINESS

14
BEST PLACES TO FIND CLIENTS

You may be able to write a blue streak, but it doesn't mean much until you have clients willing to pay for your work. I have discovered that most writers don't like to be responsible for marketing their books or their writing services. Most see themselves as creative people, and they don't like the mundane business side of the work.

I can appreciate that. I have structured my life so I can spend most of my time writing and the least amount of my time dealing with business. But I know that I can't have one without the other.

One option is to resign yourself to the business side of writing. However, the better option is to attack it was the same creativity that you use to write. Marketing can be a fertile field for your creative abilities.

The important thing is not to agonize over marketing your services. Find the line of least resistance to get the best results that meet your needs.

What are the best places to find clients? The best place is any place where you can find regular work that pays what you're worth. I'll talk about how to go about setting your fees later.

YOUR LOCAL COMMUNITY

If you want to catch fish, you need to go to the waterways where you know they live. It's best if others are already catching fish there. Your task is then to do a better job of fishing than the others. Where are the fish you wish to catch? Try these ponds.

- **Local businesses.** Not only retail stores but also manufacturing and service businesses. Everyone has a website, and you can present options to them for gaining greater visibility through content marketing. View the sites of local businesses and provide them with a free report about the strengths and weaknesses of their content. Give them a proposal for helping them.

- **Professionals.** Doctors, lawyers and other professionals in your area are constantly trying to educate potential patients or clients about their specialty. These professionals usually don't have the time to write articles. When they do, they tend to be "profession-centric." That is, they look at their specialty from their own perspective. That is not the way to build a patient or client base. Articles should be "reader-centric."

  Not only can you write fresh articles for these people, but sometimes you can simply translate what they have written into the language of the people. They become substantially more valuable to the professional when you make them more readable.

- **Nonprofits.** Most communities are filled with nonprofit organizations that have websites that need to increase or improve their public face. These nonprofits include every type of organization from local churches, to the Elks Lodge, to the local chapter of national groups like the Red Cross. They can be hospitals or local city agencies like the police or fire department. Each of them can be a profit center for you.

One of the problems with nonprofits is that they would love for you to volunteer your services. You might want to do that if you are new to content writing and need to gain some credibility. However, as a professional, you cannot afford to do very much *pro bono* work. My advice is to offer a 10%-15% nonprofit discount. Sell that as a benefit to nonprofit clients. They will understand from the beginning that you are not working for free but care about them enough to offer a discount.

You will want to fish in each of these categories. Drop your hook in the sweet spots to find clients in your community.

RELATIONSHIP MARKETING

You can ease your search for clients by emphasizing relationships in your marketing. It relieves the pressure of the dreaded "cold call." You want to find clients through your network of personal and business relationships.

You may not believe you have a network, but everybody has one. Sometimes they are not strong, and other times they will be conduits flooded with opportunity. Either way, you find good clients through your network.

I learned this the hard way. I had a great network of friends, colleagues, and clients. Then, I did something silly. I moved to New Zealand for 10 years. Yes, New Zealand was great, but when I returned to the United States, I found it very difficult to renew old relationships.

People changed occupations, changed companies, retired, died—all sorts of things. My writing income suffered drastically for over a year before I could restore it to its former level.

The best promotion is always word-of-mouth. Your job is to find creative and inexpensive ways to trigger that word-of-mouth awareness of your services.

I had developed a network in New Zealand, but it's a different economy. Their dollar was only worth about 50 cents in the conversion to US dollars That exchange rate only works in your favor when you spend US dollars in New Zealand, not when you try to spend New Zealand dollars in the US. Once I was back on US soil, it amounted to a 50% pay cut.

So, I'm sharing a valuable lesson with you. I took my original existing US network for granted. I wasn't conscious of how important it was to my income until I came back to the US.

IDENTIFY YOUR NETWORK

Where is the best place to find clients? It's among your family, friends, neighbors, organization fellow-members, business associates, colleagues, Facebook, and Twitter acquaintances and anyone else with whom you have a relationship.

Don't spend a penny on advertising until you have thoroughly exhausted every network avenue.

By the way, if you are stuck in some rural area or think you don't have a network to generate a client base, I want to remind you of the social principle known as, "Six degrees of separation."[27] That scientific principle says that people are six or fewer steps away from each other in a chain that includes the friend of a friend. Your task is to find someone who knows someone who can give you a content writing job.

REFERRALS ARE THE NAME OF THE GAME

You will identify some prospective clients as you look at the various connections on your network. That's good, and you should take those jobs when you can. However, the way your network helps the most is when *they* identify potential clients for you and refer them to you.

What is the best way to get someone to refer you to one of their friends or colleagues? There is only one way. Ask them to do it.

It is best if you did some work for the person in the network and they called a friend and told them what a great job you did. But that's not always necessary. People will refer you on the basis of your relationship with them alone.

SHOULD YOU PAY FOR ADVERTISING?

In a previous chapter, I urged you to stay away from the content mills. Some writers think that kind of work is better than nothing, but I'd say the reality is far different. The work only seems to come easy, but the content mills will kill your writing soul.

The next thought that occurs to many writers is that they buy Facebook or other targeted advertising. Is this a good way to get clients? I don't think so. It might give you a jump start, but if you try it, be very careful. You want to limit your ad spending to an initial small amount ($50 or less) to see if you get results. Then you want to evaluate the quality of clients you get.

If it works for you, you will then be in a position to spend more money on ads. But don't dump money, in the beginning, expecting huge results. It's the old story of taking baby steps to start, then running when you are able.

If I decided to advertise, where would I invest my money? Probably LinkedIn.com.[28] It provides the opportunity to reach other businesses who can benefit from, and presumably afford professional services. Again, if you go that route, do small tests and evaluate results before increasing your budget.

✳ ✳ ✳

The conclusion? You want to fish for writing jobs in the ponds where the fish live. Even though they may not have immediate work for you, try to build relationships in each of the three categories I mentioned.

Your best customers will come from your relationships. You must talk to everyone in *your* network and ask them to talk to people in *their* network.

You'll get the best jobs from the most reliable people at the highest prices through this kind of network relationship marketing.

You may not think you have a network to use to start your content writing business. But you do, no matter where you live or how few relationships you think you have.

15
HOW MUCH SHOULD YOU CHARGE?

In this chapter we are dealing with a difficult subject. I am going to do my best to answer a crucial question for you. That is, how much should you charge? In a previous chapter, I showed you some industry standard pricing. Now, I'm going to explain how you tailor your prices to your needs and those of your clients.

AVOID THE RACE TO THE BOTTOM

Before I get into dollars and cents, let me point out a reality. That is, there is always somebody willing to work cheaper than you.

I once had a client who wanted me to cut my prices. She liked me, my speed and the quality of my service, but someone contacted her who was willing to do the same job for a few dollars less.

What was my advice to her? I said, "Even with the discount you're being offered, you're paying too much. If you're talking price, I can suggest some people who will work for you at 90% less than the offer you got."

And that's true; I could have recommended some offshore people to her that would have done her work for 90% less than both the new person she was considering and me.

But I don't compete on the basis of price alone, and neither should you.

When people pay me, they are not only paying for the words on the page, but they are also paying for my:

- Speed
- Quality
- Knowledge
- Experience
- Helpful expert advice

We have a relationship. They know I'll do anything for them to help them. That's worth something.

If you want to compete on price alone, then you're welcome to do that. But know there will always be someone cheaper. When you compete on price alone, you join a race to the bottom. The one who gets to the bottom first does not win; they go bankrupt.

My clients, with a couple of exceptions over the last few decades, never shop for a better deal. They understand that I offer value for money, am dedicated, and thus they stay loyal.

HOW TO PRICE YOUR WORK

If you go to a dentist in the US, he or she will examine your teeth and make a list of all the problems that need attention. Then, the dentist will consult a standard, approved schedule that provides the price for each procedure. For example, they will add up these fees:

- Comprehensive Oral Exam, $100

- Full Mouth X-rays Intraoral-complete series, $148

- Cavity, Amalgam-two surface filling, $210

- Cavity, three surface filling, $256

- Root Canal (excluding final restoration), $964

So, you'd expect to pay $1,678 for this work if the dentist went by the book. But many dentists will adjust their fee depending on circumstances. Earlier, I pointed you to *Writer's Marketplace* and the Editorial Freelancers Association. Good stuff, but those are the "book prices," and you need to personalize them.

WORK BACKWARDS

There's another way to look at the pricing issue. You start with a certain number—the income you need or want— and divide that by the time you have available to write. You reduce that to a per word price.

Say you want to make that 6 figures I spoke about— $100,000 per year. Many writers work 2,400 hours per year. That's 8 hours x 6 days x 50 weeks per year. That's an example.

When you divide that $100,000 by the hours available, that means you need to make $42 per hour.

However, you can't write for 2,400 hours because you need sales and administrative time. That is a part of doing business, and you need to include that time in your fee.

So, for the sake of this example, let's say you can spend 2/3 of that 2,400 hours per year actually putting words on the page. That's 1,600 available writing hours. Divide that by the $100,000 and your hourly rate becomes $62.50 per hour.

Most writers don't want to sweat the so-called small stuff, but here is another important pricing tip. You need to include your business expenses in your fee. You may think that paying rent, electricity, telephone, Internet connection, insurance, taxes and all the rest are minor, but they are not. Add your fixed expenses to your hourly rate.

Your labor is not the only factor you need to consider when you price your work. Including administrative time and overhead to your writing time will increase your hourly rate, but that is the professional business approach.

However, I think it's a major mistake to try to make a sale to a client by offering your content writing services by the hour. The conversation usually goes like this:

> **Prospective Client:** "How much will you charge me for a sharp 1,000-word blog post on razor blades?"
>
> **Content Writer:** "$62.50 per hour."

Prospective Client: "How many hours will it take?"

Content Writer: "I don't know. We'll have to wait and see. Maybe two or three hours."

Prospective Client: "Have a nice day. Goodbye."

See what I mean? You need a more flexible plan to sell your content writing skills and still get a good price for it.

TRANSLATE THE HOURLY FEE INTO PRICE PER WORD

How fast can you write? Well, if you can research and write a minimum of 1,000 words per hour of quality stuff, you need to charge a minimum of 62.5 cents per word.

That price is well within the lower edge of both the retail and wholesale prices I documented in my earlier chapter on common content writing rates.

The only way to lower your price-per-word is to lower your annual income expectations or increase your writing speed.

People type about 30-40 words per minute on average, but they speak from 135 to 185 words per minute. Learn to voice write—that is using software to dictate your writing—and you become a productivity king or queen. See details about my online course on voice writing in the bonus section of this book.

By the way, lower annual income expectation is why people in India and other such nations work for pennies per word. According to research, a middle-class annual income in India is about US $1,200, That's $1,200 PER YEAR.[29] Sure, they're being exploited by clients from places like North America and Western Europe, but a few pennies look good to those folks, I guess. I feel sad for our writing colleagues in places like India and the Philippines, but it just proves my point that you can't compete on price alone.

WHEN THE PRICE SEEMS TOO HIGH

You will inevitably talk to prospective clients who will think your price is too high no matter what it is. And why shouldn't they say that? When they pay you less, their profits are more. They want to trap you into competing on price alone, and then they want to drive down your price. Here are techniques you can use to combat some common prospective client ploys.

Prospective Client: "I can get it written for half that fee."

Content Writer: "You can get it written for even less than that, but I offer a high level of competency and quality. My clients hire me because they are proud to offer my work to their site visitors."

Prospective Client: "If you write this article for me cheap this time, I'll pay more next time."

Content Writer: "I appreciate that, but I'll tell you what I'll do. Pay the regular fee now, and I'll discount your second job to celebrate our new business relationship."

Prospective Client: "If you write cheap for me this time, I'll recommend you to all my business friends."

Content Writer: "That's tempting, but I can't make a living if I sell below cost. Your friends may want the same discount."

Prospective Client: "Tell you what, if I make six sales as a result of your article, I'll pay your full price and a bonus of $100. Accept my low price now, and we'll see what happens."

Content Writer: "I hear what you're saying. My article will attract interest and have a solid call-to-action, but there are too many variables out of my control. Your sales depend on the desirability of your product or service, your competition, and your price. So, it's impossible for me to work on commission when there are so many unknown factors."

You can and should be polite with these people. But you don't need to go for their self-serving offers. Desperate writers tend to fall for these kind deals, but it is always best to avoid them.

THE BUNDLE

You can meet your income goals and not erode your prices when you bundle your services. Tell your client that you need to stick to your per-word fee, unless they commission you, and pay you, for three or more articles at the same time.

Offer a 10% discount for three, and perhaps a 25% discount for ten or more at the same time. Clients love this. Most business people offer bulk discounts, and they like getting them.

The downside for you is when they want to accept your offer but have you do the other articles and pay you, at a later time. You never want to do that. The whole point is for you to get the work and the payment now, not later. You want to get the topics and their thinking about content, as I have described, at one time and not have it dribble in. That is crucial to your success. Get the payment so you can reserve the time to do the work and not have to do it with the hope that they will pay you later.

The advantage of the bundle for you is that you are able to cut your administrative time, including the time it takes to make a sale when you get 3-10 jobs at one time. When you get paid at one time, you don't have to waste time chasing payments.

The biggest benefit for you when you are commissioned for multiple articles at the same time is that you are able to cut the time factor by researching all the articles in one session. You can break them out and write them one after another. You have "economies of scale," so bulk sales are a win for both your client and for you.

TRY CHARM

If I think I have a potentially well-paying, long-term client on the line, I sometimes try charm. From a stereotypical perspective, women content writers have a better chance of making this work than men. But charm is always an option when closing a sale with a worthwhile potential client.

One of my favorite techniques is to tell a prospective client that I can't cut my price per word. But then I say, "I'll tell you what I'll do. I won't charge you for words that are two letters or less in length. You know, all those words like 'a,' 'I',' 'to,' 'in,' 'as,' 'on.' That will cut your costs."

I say, "I can't do that on every job, but I'll do it for you this time."

That intrigues many potential clients. They often go for it. They see you're willing to work with them on price. Yet, you are protecting your business by making sure your price per word does not come under attack.

The thing you never tell your client is that you have to write those types of connector words anyway. Also, never tell your client that such words make up about 20% of all writing, so that's the discount you're offering. The reason you don't want to tell them this is because you are selling on charm and intrigue, not price. Your price-per-word remains unchanged. You are just strategically removing the number of words to make a deal.

Even though you are writing for less, you maintain your ideal hourly rate, the one that helps you reach your annual goal, by researching and writing faster. Speed up your process to compensate for the discount.

What if the client expects this discount the next time around? Groan and tell the person you value their business, but you have addictions to feed. Like eating and paying for electricity. Then offer to only charge half-price for the words that are two letters or less. You have given them some ground by doing that, but not enough to hurt you.

* * *

Remember, your goal as a business person is to maintain your professional prices. But it doesn't hurt to cajole your customers and stay on their good side without giving away the store.

If I haven't been clear before, let me confirm that you *always* want to charge per word. Not by the hour, and not by the page. Set all your prices on a per-word basis. Per-word is the only meaningful metric if you intend to make money as a content writer.

You'll discover that you can write some content quickly, so you do well. Some jobs take more time, so you do less well. But it seems to balance out. You want to stick to a price per word and then work as efficiently as you can to increase profit.

You want to set your per-word price high enough to cover not only your actual writing time, but also research, editing, revision, and your business expenses.

16
COLLECTING YOUR FEE

There's an old saying and it's a true one — "The job's not done until you cash the check." Most people don't use checks anymore, but you get the idea. The job's not done until the electronic payment hits your PayPal or bank account. Here are some of the things you can do to make sure that you get paid for your writing.

MOST PEOPLE WILL PAY WITHOUT HASSLE

Good clients are happy to find someone who can provide great online content. They don't quibble about payment.

It's those so-called online entrepreneurs, or "startups" as they like to call themselves who are often troublesome. They only want to pay you a penny or two a word, ask for a dozen revisions, then quibble about paying you. They are the people who are most likely to try to cheat you.

This may seem unkind to say, but there are two other classes of people that are problematic in my experience. I am always too busy with real estate people or lawyers. Both seem to have a sense of entitlement, as classes of people, and I have found I would rather not have my time commandeered with their demands. Are there exceptions to this? I'm sure there are. I'm just giving you the benefit of my decades of experience. I always try to have plenty of other work scheduled, so I am not desperate for their work. If I have a gap, I write posts for my own blogs or I write online courses or books like this one. The point is, you want to work with people that are not a vexation to your soul.

Normal people are almost never a problem. You have a clear understanding at the beginning, and you have a smooth transaction. That's the way it works 99% of the time.

SET YOUR TERMS AT THE START

The first rule of getting paid is to set your terms upfront. Put them in a confirmation email to eliminate any possibility of confusion.

An important part of setting terms setting your price, your work process, and your deadline. Make sure your client knows how many revisions you'll do for the money.

When it comes to revisions, one is best and two is the maximum. If your client wants changes, they should be very specific about what they want. You don't want to get involved in a time-wasting guessing game with them.

TWO WAYS TO GET PAID

What is the best way to get paid? There are two ways. You will either work on speculation or on retainer.

When you work on speculation, it means that you write the article and hope you will get paid. Your client will review the article, so they may reject it and never pay you. However, the client may still go ahead and use what you have written anyway.

Real clients don't do this, of course — just those people who don't value your work and want to pay a couple of pennies per page.

When I have a regular, ongoing, decent client, we agree that they'll pay me upon completion and they always do. It is important that you select good clients and treat them well. You want to drop clients that create problems for you.

Getting paid on retainer means your client pays you in advance in full, or at least 50%, to start the job. The amount is nonrefundable.

Occasionally a client will ask me why I get a retainer. I tell them it's for two reasons:

- It enables me to guarantee the deadline we agree upon. A retainer gives their job top priority.

- I have opportunity costs. That means I must reject other work to do their job and it's how writers are assured of a continuous flow of income.

Personally, I don't do single online content articles much anymore. I do them in batches of 12 or 24 articles. Clients post one or two each week at their own pace, but they have them available to use as they wish.

Quality clients understand that a retainer is appropriate in these cases. In fact, many clients you'll work with get nonrefundable deposits or retainers in their own businesses, so asking for one is not a problem for them.

You want to protect yourself by having a clear understanding at the beginning. That saves a lot of grief at the end.

In the writing game, you never want clients who ask you to bill them on terms. Of course, you will send an invoice by email, but generally, you'll expect immediate payment. Lots of businesses pay in 30 or 60 days, and you don't want to get involved in that. You often spend more time chasing a payment from them than you do writing for them. Writers get paid upon acceptance of the completed work, except in those cases where they get an advance.

YOUR PAYMENT INSURANCE POLICY

It's cheap insurance to remind new clients that you retain the copyright until you have been paid in full. Put your copyright notice on the article, along with the invoice number you have created for the job, on the draft you send them.

Tell them after they pay, you'll send them a "Copyright Assignment"[30] document so they can remove your copyright notice and legally post your article. With the assignment document, they own your work.

You assign the copyright to them, and they can use the article, or batch of articles, in any way they desire. When you transfer ownership, you transfer your intellectual property interests. Never sign a copyright assignment until after you have been paid.

You can protect yourself somewhat by doing this. It's not ironclad, but most clients understand the consequences of violating copyright laws.

Two quick points:

- First, you don't assign copyright if you've already signed a Work-for-Hire agreement. In that case, your client already owns the intellectual property rights in most cases.

- After you assign the copyright to a third-party, you can't use the copyrighted material yourself anymore. You can write fresh, unique content on the same topic, but you can't reuse the identical content if someone else owns the copyright.

You don't want to get involved with copyright assignments if you trust your client. When you have a good relationship with a client, you don't need this kind of insurance.

※ ※ ※

Collecting your fee is not usually a major issue when you deal with decent clients. The shady clients who want something for nothing will cause you grief, but fortunately, they are in the minority.

In most cases it works like this:

- You'll have a good understanding with a qualified client.

- You'll do the work and they may request a minor change or two.

- You make their changes, and they pay your invoice by credit card, PayPal or other electronic means.

Checks are mostly dead, so you want to avoid receiving that kind of payment if possible. Fast electronic payment is best for you.

17
HOW TO INCREASE YOUR CLIENT BASE

Once you have a few clients, you want to build on that foundation. In this chapter, and the one that follows, I want to talk about how to build a business.

The point of these chapters is the idea that if you are a writer, you want to write. There is a certain amount of administrative work that you are forced to do, but the most time-consuming aspect you want to avoid is new client development.

It takes an enormous amount of time to find good clients, so you want to find the best you can and then cultivate them.

HOW TO FIND GOOD CLIENTS

It's always funny to me—you find one of these low-paying, demanding clients who only want to pay you a few cents a word. They say the next job they have for you will pay more. They say they will recommend you to their friends.

I laugh at that one — no one wants a low-paying client and especially does not want to be recommended to his or her low-paying friends. Talk about a disaster!

So, you want to start with the best quality clients that you can get. You want to do great work for them because you know they respect what you do, are willing to pay you a respectable amount of money, and will refer you to others who will enrich you.

So, how do you increase your client base? It's a two-step process.

- You want to start with the best quality clients you can, and then
- You want to ask your clients for referrals.

Yes, I discussed this earlier, but it's such an important topic that I want to emphasize it from a slightly different perspective.

Do you see what's happening here? You are entering someone else's network. When you get a referral from a satisfied, well-paying customer, then you benefit from the existing relationship that those two people already have.

That's a powerful way to make money. That's how you increase your client base. You don't need to struggle to get work if you simply ask your satisfied clients for referrals. They'll be happy to give them to you in most cases.

Once you get referrals, you want to take good care of them when they become customers. You want to maintain a great reputation. As a writer, you do that in two key ways.

- Deliver quality content that meets the needs of your clients.

- Meet deadlines. Even if you are a great writer, you can ruin your reputation by not delivering on the promised date.

Referrals are a two-edged sword. If the word about you becomes bad through that same network, then your income will suffer.

HOW TO ENRICH YOUR CLIENT BASE

Not only do you want to increase your client base, but you also want to increase the quality of your clients.

Again, the goal is to work with a group of friendly, well-paying customers who value you, your time and your work.

You don't want to work with people who hassle you, who want you to work cheap, who are always in a rush, who want lots of rewrites, or who find some excuse to pay you slowly or not at all.

You may start with a few people like that, but you want to cut them as soon as possible. You need to review your client list every 60 days. Rank them by the amount of work they give you, how much they pay you, and how easy they are to get along with.

You want to get rid of the people at the bottom of the list. As I have said before, life is just too short to deal with people who are a vexation to your soul. Replace them with better clients by regularly asking your best clients for referrals.

You will be tempted to accept jobs from these low-list clients, but if you're going to be successful, you need to set some boundaries. Just tell the low-quality clients that your writing schedule is full each time they contact you. Don't get in a position where you are desperate for their work.

One thing I never do is write a free article so prospective clients can see the quality of my work. That's nonsense and a waste of time. If you have done work for others, give the prospective client links to that work.

If you're just starting out, you should have your own website, and have a few dozen blog posts there. People can see a sample of your writing without doing custom work for them.

Only scammers want you to write a custom article for them, in my view. If they ask 50 different writers to do a 500 or 600-word sample on a topic they request, they have enough content for their own website. They'll reject everyone's work, so they don't have to pay for it, but they'll use it anyway. You cannot build or enrich your client base when you give away your work.

* * *

To be a successful content writer, you must work at increasing your client base. You do that by getting referrals from your best clients.

If you end up as I did, you will find yourself with a couple of dozen well-paying, easy to work with clients. That's enough to supply you with a low six-figure income if you work it right.

After you have a group of good, regular, well-paying clients like this, then you take excellent care of them. You want to go the extra mile with them, even work all night if need be to meet a rare tight schedule.

That's how you grow a business. Get a good client base and take excellent care of them.

18
HOW TO INCREASE INCOME FROM EXISTING CLIENTS

Many content writers think they can increase their income by increasing their number of clients. Some even go so far as to have so many clients that they need to hire employees to write for them.

You have to decide for yourself if you want that kind of hassle. Personally, I always wanted to keep busy with my own writing and not be in the business of trying to manage a group of clients and a group of workers. To me, that takes all the fun out of it. You may think differently.

My goal has always been to get into a pattern where I can work for a stable of regular clients, as I mentioned, do the writing myself, and make six figures a year. I did that for years, and it was profitable and fun.

THE FIRST STRATEGY

How do you increase your income without getting involved with more clients or employing additional workers?

The answer is a simple one—you increase the amount of money you get from each existing client. There are three primary ways to do this.

DO BATCH JOBS

You will find sooner or later that doing single articles is not a very efficient way to work. You don't want just to wait three months to get a commission to do another single article. There's little money in that.

You need to persuade your client that he or she will get more benefits and more sales if you do a series of articles on the same or similar topic.

The fact is, this is a true statement. When the search engine spider comes through to index pages for search results ranking, it will be glad to see articles on the same or closely related topics. It gives the site what is called "authority" on that topic.

Yes, you may write one-off articles, but try to minimize that. Always suggest that you should write 3-12 articles at the same time. Your client may drip release them on their site — like two a week over 5 to 10 weeks — and both search engines and your client's site visitors love that.

So that's one way you get more money from the same client. Don't sell them one article. Instead, explain the benefits of doing a series of articles at the same time. They will get a discount, as I explained previously, and you get the benefit of consolidating your efforts.

UP-SELL YOUR SERVICES

The second primary way to increase income from existing clients is up-selling your services. You are selling them content writing, but you add services to increase income.

Frankly, you'll probably find content writing gets a little tedious after a while. You may make a six-figure income, but variety is the spice of life.

SEO Research

What kind of services can you up-sell? The first one that comes to mind is SEO services. I always insist that clients supply their own keywords and phrases, as mentioned in an earlier chapter, because keyword research is time-consuming. You can't afford to do it free.

SEO work is a specialty. You need to learn about doing it well and charge appropriately.

I'm not advising you to offer to SEO optimize your entire client site. That is an entirely different kind of technical work, not content writing. However, you can get extra SEO pay for optimizing each article you write.

Write Client Ebooks

You can increase your income from existing clients by writing an ebook that promotes the product, service or idea that your client is promoting.

If you've done a number of articles for their website, you already know a bit about their business, so writing an ebook is a fairly easy jump.

Why would your client want an ebook?

- They pay you to write it, but your client gives it away free to get customers on their email list. The money is in the list, as they say, so a free eBook that you write adds value to your client's business.

- You ghostwrite the book so your client's name goes on it as the author. That gives your client visibility and stature among his or her clients and colleagues.

- Your client can sell the ebook if he or she wishes. That could be an additional profit center for them. Clients and colleagues will say, "Hey, Jane is an authority — she wrote a book." Do you care if your name is on the book as the author? Of course not. Give the glory to your client.

A good, solid, helpful ebook is about 15,000 to 25,000 words. That's equivalent 10 to 15 online articles. But you get paid far more than your article rate. You can get far more for an ebook with the same number of words, especially if you handle the cover, create the ebook file and make it ready for people to download from your client's website or places like Amazon.

So, writing an ebook for your client is a great up-sell. That's how you increase income from your stable of good clients.

Other Profit Add-ons

When your client realizes that he or she can make money from their online mailing list, they want to start sending a helpful newsletter on a regular basis. These newsletters offer free information to clients, but they also contain a sales call-to-action.

Who is going to write that series of promotional emails? It could be you. That's a great way to increase your sales from existing clients.

Writing such newsletters requires skill. You don't want to make email newsletter subscribers mad by constant high-pressure sales tactics, so it takes some finesse to both help them and sell them at the same time. You may need to learn more about the psychology and best practices behind promotional newsletters, but as a content writer, you have the basic skills.

Also, you can write sales brochures. You can write employee guides or product safety manuals. Writers get premium prices for such documents.

Big companies like to have an official history they can publish and give to their clients. Entrepreneurs like to be profiled as the heroic figure in their company.

And so it goes. Look for opportunities to increase your writing income from existing clients.

* * *

In summary, you can increase your income from a relatively small group of good clients.

You don't need to look for new clients, you just have to be aware and meet the existing wide-ranging needs of the clients you have.

Discover client writing needs, whether they are totally aware of those needs themselves or not, and then present a proposal to do the work.

19
SHOULD YOU SIGN LEGAL AGREEMENTS?

In this chapter I want to talk about two important legal considerations. Let me make two disclaimers from the beginning. One is that I'm not a lawyer. I've been working in the intellectual property field for decades, but one thing you quickly learn is that all legal issues come down to particular cases. So, I can talk about things in general, but your case may vary. You want to check the laws and get the advice of a lawyer in your local area as it relates to your particular case.

Should you, as a writer, be fearful about consulting a lawyer? People, in general, like to avoid them for good reasons, including their high fees, but it's a sensible choice in certain circumstances. If you are planning to do something new, they often think of dozens of possible bad outcomes to thwart your dreams. Consider what they say, but make your own decision.

On the other hand, you should consult one if you are asked to sign any kind of contract. They may charge you hundreds of dollars to review it and advise you, but they may save you thousands of dollars, and lots of grief, by pointing out the pitfalls.

Lawyers are not created equal. Writer's almost always want to find an attorney that specializes in intellectual property rights, not a generalist or someone who specializes in real estate or another field.

My second disclaimer is that I don't know for certain if the issues I'm discussing here apply worldwide. They apply in many places in the United States, and I've learned over time that such laws tend to appear in one form or another around the world. Check your country, state or regional laws.

SHOULD SIGN A NONDISCLOSURE AGREEMENT?

The first issue is whether you should sign a nondisclosure agreement, commonly called an NDA.

The idea behind an NDA is that your client is going to share certain information with you and he or she does not want you to share it with anyone else. You are legally bound not to share it. There is a court case and sizable financial penalty if you share it.

So what is my policy on signing an NDA? I never sign one under any circumstances.

Of course, I never share confidential information, but I would never legally bind myself as some clients wish.

Why do I have this policy? It's because many clients think they have a unique idea — something nobody else has thought of before. But it's seldom true. I see similar ideas all the time.

If I sign an NDA on some automotive process, for example, it means that I cannot write an article for anyone else on any other automotive process that might be related, in any way, to the topic covered in the NDA. I'd put myself at risk.

If you sign an NDA you'll likely lose money because you won't be able to write, with a clear conscience, on anything even close. You never know when a client will sue you for a real or imagined breach of the NDA. So, why limit what you can write about? Why open yourself up to potential lawsuits?

My advice is never to sign a nondisclosure agreement. Your client is not paying you enough money for the grief associated with such agreements, so you just want to move on to your next client. That's my personal view.

SHOULD YOU SIGN A WORK-FOR-HIRE AGREEMENT?

If you are an employee of the company in many jurisdictions, your work product, your writing, is owned by your employer. You can't copyright it because they own it. If you reshape the material to use it in other writing projects, you could be subject to copyright violations. You write it, but you do not own the intellectual property rights in all likelihood. You have no choice in this matter as an employee.

What's the situation if you are a freelancer? If you are a freelancer and sign a Work-for-Hire agreement, it means that the person or company you signed with owns the intellectual property rights — the copyright. In fact, they can sue you if you write a similar article for which they own the rights.

Do you want to sign a Work-for-Hire agreement? Almost never. Especially when you're writing online content. The dollar value is not usually high enough to warrant it.

Also, not signing a Work-for-Hire agreement gives you leverage to get payment from a client if they try to cheat you.

Are there cases where you would sign a Work-for-Hire agreement? Yes, I can name two examples where I signed such an agreement. The first was for an installation manual for a window manufacturing company. Don't laugh about those kinds of technical writing jobs — you can pick up $25,000 or more doing them in many situations.

Anyway, the company wanted full ownership of the finished document. They paid me handsomely, and there was no other practical use for it, so I was happy to sign my rights away in that case.

Another situation involved a ghostwriting job I did. I interviewed my client and wrote his life story. Even though it was a biography in the true sense — he published it under his own name as an autobiography. I got no credit for writing the book. But that was okay. Again, I was paid handsomely for my work, and I was happy for him to have complete intellectual rights in that circumstance. His life story belong to him, and I couldn't recycle it, so I had no problem. I happily signed a Work-for-Hire agreement for him. It all comes down to individual cases.[31]

❋ ❋ ❋

You normally want to avoid signing any legal documents that restrict you in any way. A writer needs his or her freedom.

It really has to be an exceptional job with exceptional pay — something off the charts — before you even consider signing away any of your rights.

Even then, be sure to check with a lawyer. It's worth the price to have your lawyer independently review the document your client wants you to sign.

20
TAKING CARE OF BUSINESS

Content writing *is* a business, not a hobby. Even if it's a side hustle to you, a businesslike approach is essential. You want to be able to create and engender sustainable business relationships that are mutually beneficial. What does that mean?

CLIENT RELATIONSHIPS ARE KING

First, it means, as I have said, that you want to develop excellent client relationships.

- You want to avoid clients who want a single article written now and then. You can't run a real business with those kinds of clients.

- You want to find clients who are running a serious business themselves and want to use your expertise to build it online.

- Once you discover you have a good client, you want to treat them well. I'll do anything for my good clients because I realize they bring me many thousands of dollars each year. If I need more work, they refer me to their friends and colleagues.

Sure, I want my clients to respect my expertise. But I respect them too. I want to work with the smallest number of friendly clients possible to reach my annual income goals.

Content writing enables you to live a profitable and peaceful life if you do it right. That's no small thing, so developing a solid content writing business can be a good thing to do.

You get to your goals faster by developing a strong client base and treating your customers better than they expect.

KEEP TRACK OF FINANCES

Another aspect of taking care of business is watching your finances. That means several things.

- You want to be businesslike and have a bank account and do proper accounting. Don't use your personal account for your business.

- You want to track your business expenses. Money spent is money in your pocket because expenses are tax deductible.

- Get an accountant (preferably a Certified Public Accountant or CPA) to produce a quarterly Profit and Loss Statement for you each quarter. That's the only way you can know if you are making a profit.

- Pay your taxes on time. Your CPA can guide you about that.

Be aware that content writing is a business and that it can be big business. Operate your business in a professional way.

MANAGE TIME WISELY

You take care of business when you manage your time wisely. There are many aspects to that, but let me focus on one factor.

That single most important time management issue crucial to your success is this — you must keep deadlines. Don't make promises you can't keep.

Sometimes we writers bite off more than we can chew, and we pay a huge price when clients can't trust our delivery deadlines. Clients depend on us to deliver their content when you promised it. If I get behind, I work longer hours to get the job done on time. I make deadlines, not excuses.

My personal policy has always been to pad my schedule a bit, and that enables me to deliver early in most cases. Clients love that.

TAKE CARE OF YOURSELF

Some readers may think this is out of place, but I consider it a very important part of taking care of business. That is, you must take care of yourself.

I have learned the hard way that you become a better writer when you sleep well, eat nutritious food and get enough exercise. Have a social and family life outside your writing life.

I'm going to go a step further and suggest something that is beyond your physical health. When you take care of business, you also take care of your emotional health. You want a sense of tranquility as you approach both administrative and creative tasks. Two simple things that will help:

- Have an uncluttered workspace. You may not have much order in the rest of your life, but an orderly workspace will give you clarity and purpose. Get rid of the physical clutter around your workspace.

- Have an uncluttered mind. Meditation means different things to different people. Sometimes it's prayer, and sometimes it's just a time of quiet mental focus. No matter what form of mental quietness you follow, I urge you to do it before you start to write. Take a couple of minutes and clear the mental clutter from your mind and prepare to focus on your writing task.

You take care of business when you take care of clients, finances, your body, and your mental energy. When you take care of your business in these ways, you'll discover that your content writing business will take care of you financially.

※ ※ ※

Let me suggest that you do your best work when you work in a pleasant environment and lead a simple life. Some people need to complicate their life— like working with cheap, demanding clients. By promising to meet impossible deadlines. By not taking care of business.

I have been a professional writer for over three decades, and I go in the opposite direction. I want to work with people I like. I get personal satisfaction from meeting deadlines. I like doing quality research and writing content that wows my clients. I like writing fast.

So, the takeaway here is to keep your life simple. Be orderly. That's how you really take care of business and achieve content writing profits.

MEET THE AUTHOR

D.L. Hughes has been a writer, editor, and publisher for over three decades. He has written a wide range of material, including online content, documentary film scripts, and fiction and nonfiction books. He has covered stories in over two dozen countries as a journalist.

He was an editor for a national magazine, served as media director for nonprofit organizations, written or ghostwritten dozens of books, and has owned an Indie publishing company for over 25 years.

Hughes has taught at media conferences and at colleges both in the US and overseas. He was named to *Outstanding Educators of America*. He mentors fledgling writers, teaches online courses and provides personalized author services at his website, VelocityWriting.com.

BONUS SECTION

 Did you gain benefit from this book? Please take a few moments and review it at the place where you purchased it. I'd be grateful.

Thank you for reading *Content Writing Profits*. Get more value by accepting my bonus offers. VelocityWriting.com/cwp-reader-bonus/

FREE ONLINE MINI-COURSE

I offer a free course to help authors reach their writing goals. The free online course changes, but you can learn how to enroll for no cost at the link above.

ONLINE COURSE DISCOUNT

In chapter 16 of this book I mentioned my online course *"How to Speed Write Your Book with Voice Recognition Software."* The voice writing techniques I teach will help you jump to quantum speed for online content too. Click on the link above for a HUGE discount when you enroll in the course.

PERSONALIZED AUTHOR SERVICES

Need writing, editing, publishing or marketing help? See the services and the special discount I offer my readers at the above link.

LEGAL NOTICES, DISCLAIMERS & DISCLOSURES

Intellectual property is cited as follows: Sources are often credited in the End Notes section.

1. Visual content without attribution is either created or copyrighted by D.L. Hughes, used under a paid non-attribution license or in the Public Domain.

2. In cases where a Creative Commons (CC) License element is used it is noted in the End Notes section. Various CC license versions referenced in the attribution can be viewed at https://creativecommons.org/licenses/.

3. Some material is used in accordance with Title 17 of the US Copyright Act. Attribution, formal or informal, is supplied when appropriate. If you have copyright concerns, contact us via email at:

VelocityWriting@gmail.com.

4. Trademarks. All product names, logos, and brands are the property of their respective owners. All company, product and service names used are for identification purposes only. Use of these names, logos, and brands does not imply endorsement.

5. This content is not intended as a substitute for professional advice. You are advised to consult a licensed professional in your geographic region for legal, accounting, medical or other professional advice so the professional can assess your particular situation.

6. The facts and opinions are offered as a general overview of the topic, and your specific application of the information will vary. The author has made every effort to ensure the accuracy of the information in it was correct at the time of release, but there are no representations or warranties, express or implied, about the completeness, accuracy, reliability, suitability or availability with respect to the information, products or services contained in this book for any purpose.

7. Nothing in this content should be interpreted as a promise or guarantee of earnings. Any use of this information is at your own risk. Each individual's success depends on his or her background, skills, knowledge and motivation. The use of our information, products and/or services should be based on your own due diligence, which you undertake and confirm that you have carried out to your complete satisfaction.

The author makes no warranty of any kind, either express or implied, including but not limited to implied warranties of merchantability and fitness for a particular purpose, with respect to the content or embedded links. In no event shall the author be liable for any damages (including damages for loss of business profits, business interruption, errors or omissions, whether such errors or omissions result from accident, negligence, or any other cause, or other pecuniary loss) arising out of the use of or inability to use this content, even if the author has been advised of the possibility of such damages.

8. Testimonials and examples used are exceptional results, which do not, or may not, apply to the average person, and are not intended to guarantee, promise, represent and/or assure that anyone will achieve the same or similar results.

9. Some portions of this material may appear in various edited or unedited forms in seminars, other website blog posts, videos, presentations, ebooks, paperback book editions, audiobooks, podcasts and online courses written, produced and copyrighted by D.L. Hughes and branded in varying ways.

END NOTES - RESOURCES

[1] The reported number of websites vary, but this seems to be a reliable source (Accessed April 2, 2018).
   https://www.softwarefindr.com/how-many-websites-are-there/

[2] A resource that will help you measure results. (Accessed April 2, 2018).
https://www.socialmediatoday.com/news/are-you-wasting-money-how-to-measure-content-marketing-success-infographi/520754/

[3] Carol Tice hates to see people victimized by Content Mills. See some examples of her views here. (Accessed April 5, 2018).

https://www.makealivingwriting.com/confront-content-mill-owners-rates-in-person/ and

https://www.makealivingwriting.com/write-content-mills-writers-true-stories/

[4] Ibid.

[5] This is a good introduction to the issues involved in Cross-Cultural Communication. (Accessed July 12, 2017).
http://communicationtheory.org/cross-cultural-communication/

This is an older article from US Public Broadcasting, but it does a good job on highlighting key Cross-Cultural issues. (Accessed July 12, 2017).
http://www.pbs.org/ampu/crosscult.html

[6] "YouTube now lets you pay $4.99 per month to support your favorite creators." (Accessed June 22, 2018).
https://arstechnica.com/gadgets/2018/06/youtube-now-lets-you-pay-4-99-per-month-to-support-your-favorite-creators/

[7] There are three YouTube gurus I have come to value. I'm sure there are other good resources, but I recommend these:

Derral Eves is YouTube Certified and has the answers about what's happening on YouTube and how to make the most of it. He's your first stop when it comes to understanding YouTube.
https://www.youtube.com/DerralEves

Tim Schmoyer at Video Creators is the best "How to" guy out there in my opinion. His YouTube channel:
 https://www.youtube.com/VideoCreators

Video Influencers. This channel covers more than content. It also deals with tools and techniques. https://www.youtube.com/user/videoinfluencers

[8] Writer's Market schedule of fees. My numbers came from page 75. (Accessed April 5, 2018).

https://www.writersmarket.com/assets/pdf/how_much_should_i_charge.pdf

[9] Editorial Freelancers Association schedule of fees, (Accessed April 5, 2018).

http://www.the-efa.org/res/rates - "Non-specified."

Note: Both Writer's Market and the Editorial Freelancers Association update their recommended fees from time to time, so what you find may vary.

[10] There is a four-fold test to determine if you can use the "Fair Use" defense if someone challenges your use of copyrighted material. There are many commenters on this topic, and the value of what they say varies widely. It is best to go to the source to see the law and then determine how it applies to your situation. Writers tend to rationalize their use of copyrighted material by thinking it is fair use, but that can lead to trouble.
https://www.copyright.gov/fair-use/more-info.html

[11] Ecclesiastes 1:9, NIV.

[12] If you in an academic community (school or university), you are duty-bound to follow their rules. However, their rules are not the standard in the real world. Beware of the profit-making companies that are redefining the nature of plagiarism to increase their profits.

[13] "Biden Admits Plagiarism in School But Says It Was Not 'Malevolent'" NY Times, September 18, 1987. (Accessed June 14, 2018).
https://www.nytimes.com/1987/09/18/us/biden-admits-plagiarism-in-school-but-says-it-was-not-malevolent.html

14 Ibid.

15 "Biden Is Facing Growing Debate On His Speeches" NY Times, September 16, 1987. (Accessed June 14, 2018).
https://www.nytimes.com/1987/09/16/us/biden-is-facing-growing-debate-on-his-speeches.html

16 "Obama plagiarized Edwards and Patrick on the campaign trail." (Accessed June 14, 2018).
https://www.youtube.com/watch?v=wBTa6VHZlVE&t=8s

17 Chris Matthews - Obama's Plagiarism." (Accessed June 14, 2018).
https://www.youtube.com/watch?v=iq9x0AoMWQo

18 "Boston U. Panel Finds Plagiarism by Dr. King." NY Times, October 11, 1991. (Accessed June 14, 2018).
https://www.nytimes.com/1991/10/11/us/boston-u-panel-finds-plagiarism-by-dr-king.html

19 Ibid.

20 "Everything is a remix: Kirby Ferguson at TEDxFortWayne" (Accessed June 15, 2018).
https://www.youtube.com/watch?v=xRHRUNpWzAY

21 "Creativity is a remix." (Accessed June 15, 2018).
https://www.youtube.com/watch?v=zd-dqUuvLk4

22 "The 4 Steps to Getting an Idea (The Remix Method #1)" (Accessed June 16, 2018).
https://www.youtube.com/watch?v=JPJ3oy-rWUk

23 Helpful resources for trigger words to use in your titles.
http://www.copyblogger.com/trigger-words/
https://coschedule.com/blog/emotional-headlines/
https://www.incomediary.com/10-article-headline-examples-that-got-10000000-readers

24 Many people recommend Google Adwords to find key words or phrases that people use to search. It has become far less useful in recent years and I no longer recommend it. There are so-called "free" services like "Keyword Tool" but that service is limited. They want you to pay $88 per month (at

this writing) to see the frequency of various terms. These kinds of fees is another reason why you need to charge clients if they want you to SEO optimize their articles. https://keywordtool.io

There are many other SEO sites you can explore, and I recommend that you do that. As far as I'm concerned, the best place for information about SEO is Yoast. They have paid training, but here is a link to their free, and exceptionally good, basic SEO training.
https://yoast.com/academy/course/free-seo-course-seo-for-beginners/

[25] There are both free online version of Hemingway and paid desktop software.
http://www.hemingwayapp.com/

[26] The Purdue University site is an excellent source for learning or refreshing your mind about writing best practices.
https://owl.english.purdue.edu/owl/section/1/

[27] To learn more about the science behind the "Six degrees of separation" phenomena, see:
https://hbr.org/2003/02/the-science-behind-six-degrees

https://www.usnews.com/opinion/blogs/economic-intelligence/2012/07/13/networking-social-media-and-the-six-degrees-of-seperation

[28] LinkedIn,com is a business to business site. Content writers want to write for businesses.
https://business.linkedin.com/marketing-solutions/how-to-advertise-on-linkedin

[29] "How many Indians are richer than you?" Income in India (2016) 3rd Quintile average converted to USD. (Accessed July 17, 2017).
http://www.thehindu.com/data/how-many-indians-are-richer-than-you/article8551773.ece

[30] Copyright Assignment Form. This is a legally binding document. You'll probably want to check with an attorney in your region, at least the first time you use it.
http://www.copylaw.com/forms/copyassn.html

[31] Here are some Non-Disclosure resources:

Non-Disclosure Agreements - the client's side
http://www.nolo.com/legal-encyclopedia/nondisclosure-agreements-29630.html

Non-Disclosure Agreements - the writer's side
https://www.rocketlawyer.com/article/to-sign-or-not-to-sign:-what-to-do-if-asked-to-sign-a-nda.rl

Here are some additional Work-for-Hire resources:

Work-for-Hire Agreements - the client's side
http://copylaw.com/new_articles/wfh.html

Work-for-Hire Agreements - the writer's side
http://contently.net/2013/07/09/find-work/work-made-for-hire-what-it-really-means/

Remember, different laws apply in different ways in different geographical areas. Be sure to check the law in your region.

www.ingramcontent.com/pod-product-compliance
Lightning Source LLC
Chambersburg PA
CBHW031422210526
45464CB00005B/1999